DARE
TO BE YOU

DARE
TO BE YOU

INSPIRATIONAL
ADVICE FOR GIRLS

ON FINDING YOUR VOICE,
LEADING FEARLESSLY,
AND MAKING A DIFFERENCE

FROM INTERVIEWS BY
MARIANNE SCHNALL

EDITED BY
ANGELA JOSHI

TILLER PRESS
New York   London   Toronto   Sydney   New Delhi

TILLER PRESS

An Imprint of Simon & Schuster, Inc.
1230 Avenue of the Americas
New York, NY 10020

First Tiller Press trade paperback edition October 2019

TILLER PRESS and colophon are trademarks of Simon & Schuster, Inc.

For information about special discounts for bulk purchases, please contact Simon & Schuster Special Sales at 1-866-506-1949 or business@simonandschuster.com.

The Simon & Schuster Speakers Bureau can bring authors to your live event. For more information or to book an event, contact the Simon & Schuster Speakers Bureau at 1-866-248-3049 or visit our website at www.simonspeakers.com.

Interior design by Jaime Putorti

Illustrations by Georgia Morrissey

Manufactured in the United States of America

10 9 8 7 6 5 4 3 2 1

Library of Congress Control Number: 2019947283

ISBN 978-1-9821-3349-8
ISBN 978-1-9821-3350-4 (ebook)

TO MY AMAZING DAUGHTERS, LOTUS AND

JAZMIN, AND TO ALL THE OTHER INCREDIBLE

GIRLS AROUND THE WORLD:

MAY YOU DARE TO BE ALL YOU CAN BE.

CONTENTS

INTRODUCTION

In my career as a journalist and author, I have been fortunate to interview some of the most renowned thought leaders, celebrities, political figures, artists, and activists of our time, particularly on the topic of how we can empower women and girls to be leaders and forces of change. While those interviews were meant to serve the public function of having these inspiring figures share their wise insights and life lessons with the world, the experience of doing those interviews had a huge personal effect on me as well. They have been a pivotal part of my own leadership journey and evolving sense of self.

When I was a young woman, I, like so many of my peers, was thoroughly indoctrinated by the messages I received from society and the media, which whittled away at my self-esteem every step of the way. I thought my most important role was to be popular, fit in, be a perfect "good girl," and look thin, stylish, and beautiful while doing it. That resulted in not only very low self-worth and an eating disorder (the majority of girls in my friend group had them, too) but also ultimately losing touch with my true self. It would take me many years, into my late twenties, to even begin to realize this. But through my work and writing, I slowly gained insight into my own voice and power.

I had an "Aha!" moment while I was interviewing actress Jane Fonda about her book *My Life So Far* and she confessed to me that it wasn't until shortly after her sixty-second birthday, after the breakup of her last marriage, that she felt she came into her true voice and power. I related to that feeling! My first thought was: *Thank God we are both feeling centered in our power!* And then: *At thirty? At sixty? That seems much too late! How can we avoid that loss of touch with our authentic selves happening in the first place?* Those types of realizations and questions have fueled my work to inspire women and girls—so that hopefully it won't take them as long as it took me (and Jane) to find their voice and own their power.

As I have conducted countless interviews about what it will take to get more women to step into positions of leadership, one point always gets repeated: It starts with making sure girls see themselves as leaders in the first place. Our sense of self, our sense of purpose, and our voice develop when we're very young, so it is crucial for all girls to learn early on that their voice matters, that they should embrace the uniqueness of who they are and believe in their dreams and the important contributions they can offer to the world.

I have seen what is possible firsthand through raising my two amazing daughters, Jazmin and Lotus. Having grown up learning about the challenges I faced as a young woman—

combined with having the voices of incredible women like Gloria Steinem, Maya Angelou, Oprah Winfrey, Jane Goodall, Eve Ensler, and many other change makers piped through the airwaves in our house—my daughters have developed such a sturdy and centered sense of themselves. They embrace who they are, and they know they can accomplish anything they set their mind to. I am so proud of them and their desire to make a difference in the world.

That is why I created this book. Through sharing some of my favorite quotes, insights, and valuable lessons from my interviews with dozens of influential women, I want to reaffirm for girls like you that you are powerful and capable and, most important, that your voice is needed. Your dreams, your visions, your ideas, your solutions, your art, your writing, your leadership—whatever it is you feel called to bring into the world—are valued and can make a positive impact. *Dare to Be You* is a reminder to resist the negative, disempowering messages you will no doubt receive from society and the media, and to listen to and value your own voice and inner compass. Instead of being driven to fit in or conform, to be liked or be popular, or to be just like everyone else, I encourage you to embrace and celebrate the uniqueness and specialness of who you are.

When I asked activist Gloria Steinem what message she wanted to instill in girls, she answered: "That each of them is already a unique and valuable person when she's born; every human being is." Despite all the pressures that try to make girls and women measure their worth based on their looks or appearance (if only I could get back all those hours I spent feeling insecure, knowing I would never measure up to the perfect pictures I saw in magazines), what matters most is the beauty of who you are *inside*: your spirit, your smarts, and the unique gifts and insights that only you can bring to the world. You are perfect just as you are.

Ultimately, my hope is that this book will embolden you with the confidence and courage to be your full, unapologetic, fierce self—and to live a life that brings you fulfillment, meaning, and joy while also positively impacting the community and world you live in.

DARE
TO BE YOU

1

BELIEVE IN YOURSELF

Believe in yourself. No one is going to give you the tools to make you the success that you want to be, so you've got to find it inside you.

—DONNA BRAZILE

You already have everything you need to be successful. Though I remember spending a lot of time trying to reach outside of myself in order to acquire things that I thought I needed, now in hindsight, the things that made me most successful . . . the things that are my highest values are things that I had all along. And it's so ironic, but you've already got it. You are everything that you need, as opposed to operating from this feeling of inadequacy, as if we're not enough.

—TIFFANY DUFU

The way to get back to yourself is to literally get still and be alone and to drown out the voices of the world so that you can find your own way, because your own way is always right here. Glinda the Good Witch [from *The Wizard of Oz*] is really one of my greatest spiritual teachers, because Glinda says to Dorothy, "You always had it." That really is the way. You can spend all the years of your life looking outside of yourself for the answers to "Why am I here?" and "What am I really supposed to do?" but only when you are conscious enough to connect to the stillness can you really find the answers.

Open your heart, get still, ask the question for yourself, and the answer will reveal itself. There's no question you can ask for which there isn't an answer.

—OPRAH WINFREY

We worry so much about what other people think about us, and at the end of the day I just don't see how that matters so much. And obviously that's a hard conclusion to come to for most people my age, but it's just something that's always been there in me. I just really don't care what other people think.

—JULIE ZEILINGER

What is important is that at an early age, young girls have an educational environment and the family support systems in place where everything is equal to boys and that they're told early on that there is no difference in terms of their abilities and their intellectual capabilities and their opportunities. This has to be taught early. And then we have to make sure that the opportunities are there and that we don't discriminate against those girls and that we do have what it takes for girls to succeed in school.

The support that was there for me as a young girl and as a young teenager and a young mom and all, it was just always, "You're no different from this guy in terms of your ability or capacity. Just work hard and know that you're going to hit some ceilings that you've got to shatter."

—BARBARA LEE

TRUST YOURSELF

[My message for girls is] don't doubt—don't doubt what you know. Really to connect with what we know. Because that's what started happening to me around ten or eleven. Coming from all these different directions, I started to go, "Oh, maybe I'm not right. Maybe I can't. Maybe I shouldn't." You know, that thing starts to happen, and then you forget that you know! And then when the voice that knows begins to speak, you start to silence it.

—KERRY WASHINGTON

I call that harsh inner voice the obnoxious roommate living in our head. It feeds on putting us down and strengthening our insecurities and doubts. Educating our obnoxious roommate requires redefining what it means to live a life that matters, which will be different for each of us, according to our own values and goals and not those imposed upon us by society. Humor helps. What also worked was sending myself a consistent and coherent alternative message.

—ARIANNA HUFFINGTON

FIND YOUR COURAGE

Courage and *grace* and *dignity* are the three words I live by. As a child, it took courage to survive the war that I was in. As a young girl, it took courage to be true to my brown skin in a sea of white children. As a woman, it takes courage to live in a world where we are so infused with this sense of fear. It takes courage for all of us to be a woman, a mother, a sister; to be together in a society that is breeding so much fear. Fear for our freedom, safety, economy, and world. It seems to me we are living in a time in which fear is used as a tool in the media, entertainment, culture, and politics. I think right now it takes courage to live a life of hope, a life of insights, a life of family— and to not buy into this fear that we're being sold.

I believe courage is innate in all of us—all we have to do is tap it. If we just slow ourselves down enough to recognize it and tap into it. My one message is that we have more courage, more worth, and more strength than we realize.

—LOUNG UNG

It's okay to be afraid. Fear is normal and real and, in its own way, healthy. It's disingenuous for anyone to tell us that we

shouldn't be afraid of racism or sexism or bigotry or homopho-
bia or xenophobia—you know, add the "ism" that you want.
This notion that you should reject fear or reject that the outsider sensation you have isn't real is untrue. It *is* real, but you
can tackle it. And so for me the tackling of fear, the confron-
tation of fear—fear of shame, fear of disappointment, fear of
success—is okay.

—STACEY ABRAMS

If we're waiting for our fear to abate, if we're waiting for the fear
to go away for us to do the stuff that's important, we're never
going to step up. We're never going to stand up. We cannot
wait for fear to go away because it's like waiting for breathing
to go away. It's like waiting for thinking to go away. These are
core human parts of us. So courage is not the absence of fear.
It's not about not feeling fear. It's not about conquering fear. It's
about having the capacity to notice your fear, to notice it with
compassion because you're feeling fearful about something—
and something that matters to you. . . . Courage is about being
able to notice our fear with curiosity and with compassion and
still choose to take steps in the direction of our values.

—SUSAN DAVID

DISCOVER YOUR STRENGTHS

Think about your potential—what you've been given. Practice your strengths. Know your strengths because, just like in sports, we practice our strengths every single day, and we make our weaknesses adequate. If you have a strength, go for it. Zone in on that, and that will help you decide where you are going to go.

—BILLIE JEAN KING

Find out your own potentiality. Don't look to other people and put them on a pedestal; it's pointless. Find your own strength. Look to your own strengths and weaknesses, and be your own self.

—ANNIE LENNOX

In response to the sentence that begins "I can't do this because . . . ," just think about the answer. "I can't do this because I'm a woman" or "I can't do this because I'm a kid" or "I can't do this because I'm too tall or I'm too short or I'm too old or I'm too young or I'm from this country or that country." I just have to say get over it. Come on—use what you've got!

—SYLVIA EARLE

KNOW WHO YOU ARE

You have to know yourself. Sometimes we are bound by other people's thoughts because we are not sure about ourselves. But once you know yourself, it is really an expression of the biblical statement "The truth will set you free." When you know, then you are free, your mind is free.

—WANGARI MAATHAI

One of the things that is really important is getting clear about what matters most to you. . . . Most of us, unless we've taken the time to intentionally take ourselves through some kind of process of figuring out what matters most to us, we're executing based on what matters most to other people.

—TIFFANY DUFU

It doesn't work to try to be someone other than who you really are.

—ELIZABETH LESSER

Being exactly yourself is really important. And I think you should own your ambition and be who you are and not be afraid of that. Women need to have the confidence to be who they want to be and know that they're different and that's a good thing.

—KIRSTEN GILLIBRAND

I just think you really have to know

who you are—come to terms with that,

accept that, and love that, and understand

your talents, what your gifts may be,

and how to develop them.

If you're comfortable with yourself and know

yourself, you're going to shine and radiate, and

other people are going to be drawn to you.

—DOLLY PARTON

2

LOVE YOURSELF JUST
THE WAY YOU ARE

I've been traveling all these years in the world and witnessing girls and seeing their struggles and their obstacles, but also seeing their enormous resilience and brilliance and energy and realizing: What if these girls were free? What if they could be themselves? What if they weren't spending their days pleasing but were actually in their authentic beings, listening and following their own desires and voices? What would the world look like?

—EVE ENSLER

Each [girl] is already a unique and valuable person when she's born; every human being is. Inside each of us is a unique person resulting from millennia of environment and heredity combined in a way that could never happen again and could never have happened before. We aren't blank slates, but we are also communal creatures who are born before our brains are fully developed, so we're very sensitive to our environment. The question is: How to find the support and the circumstances that allow you to express what's inside you?

—GLORIA STEINEM

The message I would most want to instill in girls is: You are more powerful than you know; you are beautiful just as you are.

—MELISSA ETHERIDGE

YOU DON'T HAVE TO BE PERFECT

We need [girls] to really internalize the message that good enough is good enough. You don't need to be perfect. We're not supposed to be perfect; we're supposed to be complete. And you can't be complete if you're trying to be perfect.

—JANE FONDA

We have to stop beating ourselves up for not doing everything perfectly.

—SHERYL SANDBERG

THE TRUTH ABOUT BEAUTY

I always thought that people told you that you're beautiful—
that this was a title that was bestowed upon you, that it was
other people's responsibility to give you this title. And I'm sick
of waiting, people! The world is pretty cruel to women, in what
it considers beautiful and what it celebrates as beauty. And I
think that it's time to take this power into our own hands and
to say, "You know what? I'm beautiful. I just am. And that's my
light—I'm just a beautiful woman."

I've done this, and it has changed the way that I carry myself,
changed the way that people respond to me, and changed the
way that I feel. It really improves *everything*! Because your
psyche responds to it, like this is truthful.

I think that [beauty] is just a feeling of goodness and happiness and that you don't have to change anything. It's about
being content and not having to fix anything or change anything or do anything—that we are perfect as we are. It's just
being as you are.

—MARGARET CHO

CULTIVATING A HEALTHY BODY IMAGE

We grow up being told, "Be a good girl." When you're told to be a good girl, that assumes that we're not inherently good and that we have to get rid of whatever is bad, so that we will become something that we're not inherently. And for girls it becomes attached to their bodies. . . .

If girls are in inauthentic relationships, they are more apt to have eating disorders. Eating disorders don't represent a lust for food. They represent a loss of authentic self. It's when there's something about our lives and our relationships to ourselves and others around us that is inauthentic, and we're trying to fill an emptiness. That's what I think it's really about. It's a spiritual and emotional hole that we're trying to fill with food. And so it's important that if you do suffer from an eating disorder, to find help.

            —JANE FONDA

I think we should treat eating disorders with the same kind of graveness and seriousness as cancer, because it is a disease and it can be terminal. And it's something that stays with you and eats you up from the inside. And I feel really worried about young women, especially in the world that we live in. Especially with the online culture that's directed at actresses' bodies and women's bodies—it's an all-out war.

When young women's bodies are criticized in the media, it sends a message out there that we are somehow *wrong*, and if I can shield young women from that message and somehow protect them, that's just become my life mission of late because I've suffered so much from eating problems. I've been in that place where nothing was satisfying to me and I was really unhappy with my own body and my own body image.

What's sad is that I spent most of my youth thinking that, and now I'm so disappointed when I look back at pictures of myself in my twenties and my teens, and it seems that I really hated my body and I hated the way it looked. And I look back and I see a really beautiful girl, and I missed it. I don't want women and girls to miss out. It's such a painful thing to come to this realization later in life, that this is what we look like. This is it. You have to enjoy and accept it; the only other choice is that misery, but that is a choice—you don't have to feel that. Learning that—kind of growing out of feeling miserable and growing out of what society's idea of beauty is and bringing into it my own idea—really is the way to solve that problem within ourselves.

—MARGARET CHO

The key to success and fulfillment is self-esteem—self-esteem, confidence, and a healthy body image. I don't know a girl, teenager, or woman—no matter how smart, how feminist, how educated, how cool, how sequestered in the country, how raised by feminist parents—I don't know one who doesn't have at least three-quarters of her thought process sucked up by how fat or thin she is.

So when you have a whole gender, when you have most of the female population, concentrating on something that ultimately means nothing, it usurps the time they might be dreaming of becoming, perhaps, the president of the United States.

—KATHY NAJIMY

I think the degree to which we love our bodies and celebrate our bodies and eat well and are healthy and all of that, the more we enter the world.

—EVE ENSLER

BE YOURSELF

Just be what it is that you are, and that is *just fine*. You don't have to be what you're not in any way. Live that and live that fully, and that is where you discover ecstasy. You can't really have ecstasy as something other than yourself.

—ALICE WALKER

[Girls will know their own worth] by having a relationship with themselves and liking themselves and accepting themselves and believing in themselves. The most important relationship in life is the one you have with yourself. That's number one. It's the only thing that matters.

—DIANE VON FÜRSTENBERG

YOU DON'T HAVE TO CONFORM

Our society is so critical of everybody. People are used to always wanting to bend; they are used to having to bend themselves to fit into whatever space they're in, and it's a thing you learn from the time you are little, so un-learning that is difficult. We've basically been trained and told that we need to be like everybody else and we need to fit in, so getting people to understand that they don't have to be like everybody else is a challenge.

—LUVVIE AJAYI

Girls are pressured to shave and pluck and obsess and wear clothes that maybe aren't authentic to their taste . . . because of images in the media and on the Internet—a car commercial, an ice cream commercial, or a poster ad for jeans. We get assaulted every single day by billboards, magazines, television shows, and films telling us there is one way to be. And usually the quest to conform takes up our time and, all too often, our lives.

—KATHY NAJIMY

The more powerful women get, the more the world intervenes at pre-adolescence to say, "Guess what? You are going to be judged by your body." I'm looking at my feisty eight-year-old granddaughter and seeing how much the world is coming in on this confident, brilliant little girl—about her hair, about how she looks.

I kind of disagree with some of the stuff that's been written and done lately about girls, because girls are not mean—they mean to have power. But when the country, the culture, the people around them keep talking about how you get power one way, which is to be a good girl—to look good and to be good—then it's hard to keep the idea that you could be a tough little president. And frankly, the more power women get, the more it starts coming at them. I think that's starting to change, but we have to remember that culture keeps coming back at you and pushing it in the other direction.

—MARIE WILSON

Why can't all different types of women be considered beautiful? Our society, for the most part, when it deals with or talks about women's bodies, is *wrong*. You don't have to be a size zero. You don't have to be like one of these bone-skinny actresses. You *can* be, if that's how you naturally are, but you don't have to strive for that.

—MARGARET CHO

We're constantly talking about calories and the media's portrayal of women, but I feel like we rarely really get into the depths of how epidemic this issue [of body image] is and how completely unacceptable it is. Why do we continue to accept that this is how it's always going to be? Is this normal? Is this okay? No, it's not normal. We don't have to accept this. There's nothing inherent about women that we walk around hating our bodies all day. This is not only unacceptable, it's also unnatural.

—COURTNEY E. MARTIN

It takes courage to step out of your skin, to step out of your role, to step out of society's roles for you. Courage is when you dare to be yourself, in whatever ways you want to be—to not be afraid, to just do it.

—LOUNG UNG

3

SEE YOURSELF
AS A LEADER

When we're teenagers, we are pure passion—we're open, we're rebellious, we're questioning—and there's enormous energy that slowly becomes shut down and censored and denied and questioned and ridiculed. If we were to really support that energy and unleash that energy, I think we would have a new wind healing the world.

—EVE ENSLER

At the age of seven, like 30 percent—across the board, boys and girls—want to be president. And then at the age of thirteen, the numbers completely skew. You have one girl for every nine guys that want to be president.

We're in a rut in our country; I feel like we're stuck. We give so much power to beauty and not enough to talent and brains and leadership when it comes to women and girls.

I think girls and women are our heroes, and they need to start seeing themselves as our heroes and to come help us out of the mess that we're in.

—JENNIFER SIEBEL NEWSOM

Young girls are not taught to want to lead. Wanting to lead and wanting to be powerful and wanting to be in leadership positions are seen as negative qualities in women that are really crushed from an early age in our culture. Anyone you talk to in organizations that work to get more women into politics, they'll tell you that women don't run for office at the same levels that men do because they're taught to think that they're not qualified.

—JESSICA VALENTI

It starts young: Girls are discouraged from leading at an early age. The word *bossy* is largely applied to girls, not boys. I think we need to expect and encourage our girls and women to lead and contribute.

—SHERYL SANDBERG

There are multiple levels of leadership—

your leadership in your own family, your

community, how you lead your life, how you

present yourself in the world as one who is willing

to use what you have to give to others. That, to me,

is the defining meaning of what

it takes to be a leader.

— OPRAH WINFREY

SEVEN LEADERSHIP LESSONS FROM REMARKABLE WOMEN

1. EMBRACE YOUR POWER

What is the girl self? It's the part of us that's passionate and compassionate and associative and intuitive and emotional and resistant. And from the time *all* of us—men, boys, and girls—are born, we're taught that the worst thing you can be is a girl. That to be a leader you should never be a girl. To be a man, you should not be a "girl." To be a woman, you can't be a girl, you know? It must be pretty powerful to be a girl if everyone's taught not to be one, right?

If you look at girls themselves around the world, they are such a potent force for change and good, for questioning, for disrupting, and for resisting, and yet they are under siege in so many places. Everywhere. Whether they're being told that they should starve themselves to please the fashion setters, or whether they're being told to cover up or shut themselves down.

I think that which makes us powerful and strong has been what we are most criticized for. And my whole life I've been told that I'm too emotional, too extreme, too dramatic, too intense, too alive—and I started to think, *What if I actually saw that as my advantage and saw that as my strength and saw that as my gift?*

—EVE ENSLER

We are more powerful than we realize. Together people create culture, and so we can re-create it.

—JENNIFER SIEBEL NEWSOM

If we can involve young people who are going out in the world as the next politicians, the next lawyers, the next doctors, the next teachers, the next parents, then perhaps we'll get a critical mass of youth that has different kinds of values.

—JANE GOODALL

Three words: Know your power. You can have role models, but be yourself. Young women may want to have mentors and may want to emulate others for what they have done, but I would encourage them to know their own power, understand who they are, and know what works for themselves in terms of timing, their life, their choices, and the rest.

—NANCY PELOSI

2. LEAD IN YOUR OWN AUTHENTIC WAY

In my opinion, the most important thing as a woman leader—and I learned this early through a whole bunch of great women who were in my life, and men, I have to say—is that if you have a position of leadership and power and you don't use it in a different way, then you're wasting it. When people used to say to me when I was the first woman president of PBS, "Does that mean that as a woman you're going to be a different kind of president?" And I would say, "Well, I hope so! I *want* to be a different kind of president."

And I think if we back away from that, that's why the progress doesn't count as much as it should. Because if we took every step, and we figured, "Okay, I may not change the world here, but *I'm* going to do this *my* way," and we do it as a mother, as a wife, as a daughter—all the experiences of life that we bring to something as a woman—then that's going to naturally mean we're going to do that job differently. If we all did that in every place we are—starting with being president of the senior class, starting with being your school editor, on the cheerleading squad, on the soccer team, whatever—we're going to lead differently.

—PAT MITCHELL

3. TRUST YOUR INTUITION

I really do believe that women have an intuitive sense, which is very important in leadership. If you have a vision and you have knowledge and you have a plan, you know what decision you need to make intuitively. And that confidence is contagious. If you act in that decisive way, people will have confidence in you. And they'll follow your lead.

—NANCY PELOSI

All of us know not what is expedient, not what is going to make us popular, not what the policy is, but in truth each of us knows what is the right thing to do. And that's how I am guided. . . . When I want to think about what would be the right thing to do, the fair thing to do, the wise thing to do, I can just think of my grandmother. I can always hear her say, "Now, sister, you know what's right. Just do right!"

—MAYA ANGELOU

4. KNOW THAT YOUR IDEAS ARE VALUABLE

There's the Greek myth of Cassandra. Cassandra was one of the most well-known Greek goddesses, and her story was that she was endowed with the gift of vision, foresight, and wisdom, but she was also cursed by the gods in that no one would listen to her. And, in a way, all women have been playing out that myth of Cassandra from the beginning of time. We know some really important things for humanity, but we have not been listened to, and as a result, we've gathered some unfortunate behaviors where the way we express what we know isn't respected.

Over my years in leadership I've learned, first, to trust that what I feel, know, and see is of value. And, second, to learn a way to speak it in such a way that it's listened to and acted on.

—ELIZABETH LESSER

5. DO NOT BE AFRAID TO STAND ALONE

I tell young people: Be passionate about what you believe in, and do not be afraid to stand alone, because you may find yourself in a position one day where you have to stand alone. When you know it's that important, don't be afraid. That doesn't mean it's easy; it isn't. But if you feel strongly about a certain position and certain values or a certain view, and if you believe you're right, then you should be able to stand alone.

—OLYMPIA SNOWE

Somebody has to be first, and it might as well be you.

—CAROL MOSELEY BRAUN

6. REMEMBER THAT YOU DON'T HAVE TO DO IT PERFECTLY

In terms of leadership more generally, there are still gender stereotypes that encourage women to remain silent. I see this in the classroom all the time, even at the collegiate level, where boys are constantly the ones raising their hands to say just about anything, and young women either don't really speak at all, or only speak when they feel they have some perfectly formulated answer and something really valuable to say. They don't participate in the same way, and they don't put themselves out there in the same way, and I think that's a huge factor in determining if they want to become a leader or not.

Women are still socialized differently than men at a very young age. We're still praised for being pleasing and non-confrontational in a way that men are not. And as we get older, we're also socialized into this perfectionist standard—whether it's unattainable beauty standards or academic standards. I think women look at leadership as requiring a kind of perfectionism that men really don't. And that's the thing I see more than anything else, more than looking at women leaders and thinking, *That's not something I want to do*. I think women my age look at it and think, *That's not something I'm good enough to do, that I have to be so much smarter than I already am, I have to be so much more accomplished*. Whereas guys my age tend to cut themselves a little more slack and think that they can take on leadership with the same qualifications.

—JULIE ZEILINGER

We've been socialized—girls have been taught to be perfect and boys have been taught to be brave. Don't let yourself think that you have to be perfect.

—BILLIE JEAN KING

7. GET STARTED

You don't have to wait to become a leader. You can start right now. What do you see in the world that doesn't seem right, feels unfair, needs to change? Learn more about it. Speak up—at school, at home, with your friends. Brainstorm solutions. Then get going. You don't have to wait until you're an expert or have your degree—or even until you're old enough to vote.

Greta Thunberg is sixteen years old, and she's already a global climate activist. Emma Gonzalez and her classmates at Marjory Stoneman Douglas High survived the attack on their high school to become passionate gun-control advocates. Their tools belong to you—your voice, your experiences, your time. Go to a march. Share a petition. Start a school club. Make public art with a message. Help register voters—and when you're old enough, vote in every election you can.

You can make a difference, and you can help others do the same. That's what a leader does: She helps us build a better future together. You got this. Now get to work!

—SHERYL SANDBERG

4

RESIST NEGATIVE
MESSAGES IN THE MEDIA

LIKE IT OR NOT, THE MEDIA
IS A PART OF LIFE

The media is where we get our ideas of what is normal, what is okay, what is possible for us, what we can become. For all the time that human beings have been on earth, we have been sitting around a campfire telling our stories. And if one person could not tell their story, people didn't learn from them, and the circle was incomplete. The media is our campfire.

A whole set of possibilities, problems, dreams, and realities are just not present unless we are equally represented in the media.

—GLORIA STEINEM

The media is the most important and powerful force we have. It defines us. It tells us who we are. It tells us our role in society. It tells us what matters; it tells us who matters. It also tells us who has power. Every image that you see, every story that you read, every frame that an editor puts into a film shapes the story, and if women and people of color are not represented in those stories, it makes us not represented in society.

—JULIE BURTON

We know media have this profound impact, that the narratives we see, mostly in entertainment media, shape who we're supposed to love, who we're not supposed to love, who the good guys are, who the bad guys are, what our values should be, and how we should spend our time. They basically shape our core identity.

More diverse images of women in media would lead to a revolution of identity and leadership if millions of little girls grew up thinking of themselves as fully capable, ambitious human beings.

—CAROLINE HELDMAN

The media creates thought—everybody's consciousness, you know? People don't get their consciousness from anything else these days. The media tells you what's important.

—CAMERON DIAZ

There is probably nothing more relevant in our lives today than the way in which the media is portraying women, representing our lives, talking about us, or not talking about us.

—PAT MITCHELL

BE AWARE OF HOW THE MEDIA
MAKES YOU FEEL

Become conscious of what the media is doing to you—how it's making you feel like you're supposed to be "this" kind of a girl, sexy and thin and so forth.

The media is the major part of what creates our culture, and culture is what creates consciousness, and culture is the lens through which we view the world and view our roles as men and women and how we are supposed to behave. If the media shows women in a degrading, demeaning way, if violence is not taken seriously, if female candidates are covered in the context of how they look and what their hair is like and how they're dressed as opposed to how the male candidates are covered, this has an impact on women and girls. It's not always conscious, but it can't help but make us feel, somehow, that we don't count as much.

Adolescents [should be] conscious of the fact that what's happening to them right now, along with all the body changes, is they're forming the identities that will take them through the gateway into adulthood, and they should do it consciously. What kind of person do you want to be? What kind of values do you want to represent? Write them down so you can internalize them more easily and focus on them, and then, every now and then, go back to the list. Are you being those things? Are the friends you've chosen to hang with people who encourage you to be those things? The focus is not *what* you want to be when you grow up, but *who* you want to be. The more conscious we can make them of that, the healthier they'll be, and the more they'll be able to handle what comes along the way.

—JANE FONDA

I think everything that influences girls comes from the media to some degree. I mean, where are eating disorders learned? In the images that the media perpetuates—whether it's advertisements or TV shows or movies or the images of what you're supposed to look like.

—EVE ENSLER

Women often don't look like they're presented in the magazines, even in magazines that are made for other women. The images don't coincide with the reality of who we are. It's such a difficult thing to endure that. How do you maintain a healthy self-esteem when you don't have images around you that reflect you? I can't stress enough how damaging it is—the constant barrage of thinness and youth and a racial, monochromatic idea of what beauty is. It's really a tough thing for women. I don't know how girls survive.

There's even a problem in language, there's a problem in the media, there's a problem in society. There are just so many things challenging girls and women in their search for power and strength that we need to do all we can to help that along.

—MARGARET CHO

Looking back on my own experience, so many more girls were so much more vocal in fourth and fifth and even sixth grade, and there was a lot of equality in the classroom at that point. It was around the time that young women began to realize that there were these different standards—beauty standards in the media that had a huge impact on the way we viewed ourselves and reconsidered our relationships with others. It's hard for young women to look at the way other women are objectified in the media, how they're photoshopped to perfection, and not feel that we have to live up to this perfectionist standard. This is a phenomenon that just doesn't occur for our male counterparts. And once we realize that there's a perfect image we're not living up to, we begin to question ourselves in all aspects of our lives. It starts with reconsidering our bodies, but it really feeds into everything that we do. And I think that negative body image has a huge impact on the rest of our lives.

—JULIE ZEILINGER

Are the media partly culpable for their portrayal of women and its effect on girls' and women's low self-esteem and therefore lack of success? I say yes. From salacious music videos to billboards solidifying that your value is your sex; to one-dimensional, diminishing roles for women; to body and appearance scrutiny; to lack of scope and truth in portraying women's history; to magazines, newspapers, news shows, and TV shows that demean, insult, and exclude women; to music that promotes violence and abuse against women as hip and relevant; to the lack of adventurous, intelligent, and proud girl characters in our children's TV programming; to oppressive stories in animated films and fairy-tale books; to the consistent message that the goal is being desired and swept away by the prince; to the notion that the golden ring (literally) is finding someone to marry and support physically and emotionally so that then your husband can thrive and therefore take care of you. What you are left with is a bunch of capable and fierce but unencouraged—or excluded, misguided, and marginalized—girls and women.

—KATHY NAJIMY

I feel like the media is the first thing that people talk about, but it's just one of several places where girls are going to encounter messages about how strong or authentic they're really permitted to be. To me, it just means that, on some level, girls are going to internalize this. And that's not always a bad thing, as long as they can be critical of it, too. That means you can enjoy some of the media, but you also have to be critical of it, and you have to take from it what makes sense to you and leave the rest.

—RACHEL SIMMONS

DON'T GIVE IN TO THE PRESSURES FROM THE MEDIA

We women are told everywhere we turn—in newspapers, radio, television, magazines, books—that we are imperfect in so many ways. Be it our appearance, relationships, or personalities, there seem to be so many things terribly wrong with us. But how can there be that many things wrong with us and yet here we are? We've got to sit down sometimes and look at what's right and know that what's right is not anything that the world out there can dissect—it is wholly what is in you.

—LOUNG UNG

I'm speaking as someone who fell victim to all the "I'm not good enough, my breasts aren't big enough"—all that kind of thing. We need to inoculate girls against the media, until we can change the media. Help them understand what the media is doing: playing with our brains, filling us with anxieties. . . . If you can politicize what the media does and what the fashion magazines do, it's easier for girls and boys to step back and be a little less vulnerable to it.

—JANE FONDA

DO YOUR PART TO IMPROVE THE MEDIA

Representation matters. The images we see of women and girls on television and on the Internet matter. So we can't be passive. When are we going to start to take the power that we have as consumers of media and demand that it be different?

—PAT MITCHELL

The media is the purveyor of dominant values, and you have to fight with [the media] to change. It does change, slowly, but it does change.

—GLORIA STEINEM

Girls are continually besieged with the message of insecurity. The first level is insecurity: "You're too fat, too thin, too tall, too short, your breasts are too big or too little, etcetera." Step one is to convince you that you have a problem. Then the second level moves right in and says, "But we have advertisers who have *just* the thing that will address your problems." That's how the media makes its money, and the women's movement has been critiquing that for a very long time.

There's some good news on that front, though, in that girls are now taking a lot of the fight into their own hands. There are the two girls who confronted *Seventeen* magazine about airbrushing and about too-thin models. There's a number of young teenage women who have started petitions—it's so much easier now, to start a petition on, say, Change.org—and then suddenly these petitions are tweeted about, and they grow like wildfire. And so, in a sense, girls are picking up the cudgels themselves now, more and more, and getting support from other girls for doing so.

—ROBIN MORGAN

There are studies out that the more media girls consume, the more insecure they are, the lower their self-worth and their sense of power and ability. And the more media boys watch, the more confident and aggressive they are in their behavior.

The media has been sending really limiting messages to our boys about their value being power, dominance, and aggression, just as the media has been sending really limiting messages to our girls about their value lying in their youth, their beauty, and their sexuality.

We have this tremendous opportunity to rewrite that narrative and create a narrative that's more inspiring and empowering and reflective of who we all truly are. It starts with conscious consumption and with recognizing our power, as citizens, to stand up and speak out—really demanding more, expecting more, and writing letters to those who are contributing to a culture that's so demeaning and disrespectful toward women. And just not being afraid. So many people are afraid to speak out; they're afraid to ruffle feathers. And we have to. We're in this together. We've really got to start holding people more accountable.

—JENNIFER SIEBEL NEWSOM

For the first time in a long time, women are understanding that we do have power and that we need to learn to exercise it, and of course we need the media in order to give us the platform.

—MAXINE WATERS

The media should reflect America, and we're a huge diverse patchwork of people with different life experiences, different perspectives, and with differences economically, geographically, ethnically, and religiously. We have different races, different genders, different gender identification, so in order to tell the story of America, you have to let Americans—*all* Americans—be the storytellers.

There's a lot of progress that's yet to be achieved, and we have to keep focused, and we have to continue to figure out how we move from activism to action, and how we actually create a culture that is receptive and positive for everyone.

—KATIE COURIC

5

IT'S NOT YOUR JOB TO
PLEASE EVERYONE

Girls at adolescence have to be encouraged to not turn into pleasers. They have to be encouraged to hang on to their authentic self.

—JANE FONDA

It occurred to me that the people I was trying to please and the results of being inauthentic and playing small weren't ultimately fulfilling. I'm kind and fair, and I believe in justice and fairness within an inch of my being, but the nice, pleasing part is just boring to me. And it's a waste of time. I feel like you can be kind, just, and fair without having to worry whether every single person likes you. You come to a point in life where you just say, "It's none of my business what people think of me. It's my business how I act, and am I acting in a way that I respect?

Am I living in my skin?" Life is too short. You have to be willing to let go of some of the other things to move toward your authentic self.

—KATHY NAJIMY

My message really is in making the choices you want to make in your life—they really have to be yours. You have to feel them in your own spirit. And if you're always trying to please everybody around you, all you end up being is twisted into the shape of a pretzel, because, "Today I'm with Sally Sue and I have to be this way so she likes me, and tomorrow I have to be another way because I'm going to be with this group of people." If you do that enough, you'll end up not even knowing who you really are. So have the courage to be who you really are, no matter where you are.

—JODY WILLIAMS

[In my teenage years] I wish I'd known that it was okay to say "no"—that "no" is a complete sentence.

—JANE FONDA

We have to actually trust girls and stop telling them that they have to be someone other than who they are. One of the things I'm discovering is that the more girls feel confident in themselves, the more they are able to express who they really are. We have to create situations where girls find their own voices. We have to help girls find activities that fulfill their deepest selves. If you live in a society that tells you your whole point is to be pretty and skinny, then you'll spend your days working to achieve that. But if you're brought up in a world that tells you that your point is to make the world better and to contribute and to transform consciousness, then you will work on achieving that.

—EVE ENSLER

I've tried to do some reflection about [where I got my confidence and leadership abilities]. And I try to think back to myself as a little girl. I certainly didn't feel powerful. I felt very power-*less* and very trapped. But whatever it was that motivated me to fight back against that—or to push past that is maybe a better way of thinking about it—there must have been some sort of inner strength and resilience. But I've had lots and lots of periods of self-doubt and, by the way, lots of periods in which I conformed, in which I took the path of least resistance. I like to think those were the shorter periods of my life, and they certainly weren't the most satisfying; they were the *least* satisfying in every way.

I have that pleasing gene, like every other woman I know. If I had been able to suppress that a little earlier in my life, I'd be a lot stronger leader today than I am. It took me a long time to get to the point where I realized I didn't have to please everyone. It's one of the aspects of our personality that we develop. But the strength, the inner strength, really came from knowing that I couldn't rely on anyone other than myself.

—PAT MITCHELL

Part of the way I ran my campaign [for governor of Georgia] was launching the conversation that said, "I'm going to be wholly who I am. I'm not going to compromise. I'm not going to change my hair. I'm not going to change my skin color. I'm not going to change my gender. I'm not going to compromise who I am to accommodate your expectations of what I'm capable of."

What's inappropriate is ever allowing someone to wield their expectations of you as a weapon, when they use who you are against you. That's the place where I push back. . . . I never allow it to seep into my internal sense of self and weaken who I am. And people try. It's hard. It's hard to push back. And I have to remind myself that I am more than this person's low expectations of me.

—STACEY ABRAMS

Most girls spend so much of their lives pleasing somebody, whether it's fashion setters or their girlfriends or boys; they go too fast when they don't want to go fast. So much of our life is spent trying to make someone happy other than ourselves, and the verb "to please" has robbed girls and robbed all of us of our greatest energy and creativity. It has prevented us from taking risks, prevented us from speaking the truth, and prevented us from standing up against tyranny and war and oppression because we're afraid of being exiled. If I was going to say anything to girls, it would be to find a new verb. Dance, resist, invent, create, envision, protest—but stop pleasing.

—EVE ENSLER

6

VALUE YOUR INTELLECT AND EXPLORE YOUR INTERESTS

Being *interested* is more important than being interesting. If you try to learn something every day and you stay interested, you're going to be an interesting person and you're going to continue to grow.

—JANE FONDA

It's cool to be smart. . . . Girls have to fight against a lot of the same stuff we did growing up—peer pressure, exploitation, etcetera. But what worries me the most is this trend that caring about something isn't cool. That it's better to comment on something than to commit to it. That it's so much cooler to be unmotivated and indifferent.

—AMY POEHLER

Hang out with people who make you feel smart, not dumb. That's crucial. Because if they make you feel dumb, they're not supporting you, and they're not helping you. It isn't that we're right or wrong. It doesn't have to do with being right all the time, but if you have consistency of support from people who value your opinion, it will help you to value your opinion.

—GLORIA STEINEM

I remember when we were looking at the STEM [Science, Technology, Engineering, and Mathematics] fields and why more girls don't go into STEM. [We found that] even when they're in junior high, when they're making those decisions about what they want to do with their lives, and even if they are gifted in the areas of science and math—women or junior high girls—when they're asked, "What do you want to do?" they quite often think about careers in terms of making a difference and being a part of the team, and they don't see those fields— the science, technology, engineering, and math—leading to that type of career.

We talk about America being a land of opportunity, but a lot of times we don't even know what those opportunities are. I would encourage young women to just go explore. Take advantage of the internships and the fellowships and go travel and explore what's out there before you make your decision, and see where you really find your passion and where you find fulfillment.

—CATHY McMORRIS RODGERS

If we want all of our workforce, all of our great minds, focused on solving *all* the problems we need solved, we need to have more women interested in STEM. So I support legislation that can hopefully help teachers inspire young girls in their grade-school years and to teach them why being good at math and science can help people, because that's what girls want to do. More often than not, they want to have an impact on the community, and if you're good at these subjects, you can actually accomplish that.

—KIRSTEN GILLIBRAND

Girls are being taught at every turn that their looks are their value. The first thing people say to a girl is a comment about her appearance—what she's wearing and how she looks. Honestly, there is nothing wrong with compliments or looking good. I like to look nice and wear fun clothes. I compliment people on their shirt or shiny hair. I think, *Good for you!* Shiny hair and nice earrings! I'm not against women or men looking great. But it becomes a problem when the praise of girls is almost exclusively directed at their appearance, their bodies, and their makeup, when it seems to be the only value we put on them. When the first and only praise directed at my daughter (since she was a toddler) was, "You are so pretty!" how can that not stick as being the most valuable thing about you? I always try to add, "And smart!" We learn from birth that prettiness, thinness, and being attractive to boys are the prize, the golden ring, the purpose and value of our life. And from that comes insecurity, addictions, eating disorders, and a warped disregard for all else women and girls have to offer.

—KATHY NAJIMY

I'm raising two girls, and I say to them, "I need you to be strong *and* soft. You can be smart *and* beautiful. You can dress well and be a woman. You can be feminine! You can be all of these things, and even though you may think they sound contradictory, they're not."

That's a really good thing we can teach young girls—that if you're twenty pounds overweight, you're not dumb, you're not *not* beautiful, you're not *not* strong. And the more we give each other examples of that, the more honest we are with each other, the little bit easier it is to use our voices and step out.

—MARIA SHRIVER

When other people laughed at me and called me dummy, [my brother] said, "Don't worry about them calling you a dummy. You're smarter than anyone here!" And he was absolutely right! He told me that I was very intelligent and that I had to depend upon myself. He knew more than most people, and if he said I was very intelligent, I believed him. That was a big gift.

—MAYA ANGELOU

I am "Auntie" to many nieces and my girlfriends' daughters. We have this rule among ourselves: Every time somebody tells a child how cute and beautiful she is, one of us in the inner circle has to say four other things. That the child is interesting, curious, observant, detail-oriented, smart, clever, etcetera.

As a girl, I was curious, and interested in bugs, and followed my brothers as they flirted with girls, and I petted frogs—all those traits that others thought made me a troublesome, bad girl, but my father thought it made me clever. This stayed with me. And it's made all the difference in how I view myself.

—LOUNG UNG

7

PAY ATTENTION
TO YOUR HEART

T he heart has gotten a really bad rap. We're constantly belit-
tling the heart and putting the heart down and saying that
emotions can't be trusted and facts and data are what's important. Here's what I think: Both are important. And you can
have all the data you want, but if your heart isn't engaged and if
your being isn't connected to what you're doing, nothing's ever
going to change. There are all these studies being done about
the intelligence of the heart and how much the heart knows
and how we devalue it and undermine it. But my heart has led
me into the best things.

We are emotional creatures, and it's crucial, particularly in
the time that we are living in, that we're emotional creatures,
and that we respond to things with our heart. And not *only* our
heart, and not insanely or without analysis or thought, but I
think the missing *piece* right now is that passion, that outrage,

that complete empathy and complete compassion that really motivates you to go beyond and break out of the box to change things.

—EVE ENSLER

Girls are experiencing a loss of emotional intelligence, essentially an erosion of being able to know how you feel and take seriously how you feel, and then, of course, to be able to *say* how you feel. I believe one of the strongest interventions with girls is helping them take seriously their own thoughts and feelings. Authorizing girls to have their thoughts and feelings—really helping them to see that their perspective is valuable, and even if they're not going to be successful at getting what they want, that how they think and feel is all right.

—RACHEL SIMMONS

Emotional intelligence to me is a big part now of what feminism is going to include and give as a gift to the world. [Women] are emotional creatures, and emotions will save the world. Love will save the world. Passion will save the world. Communication between human beings, knowing what you feel—this is what we need right now. Everyone needs to be emotionally intelligent.

—ELIZABETH LESSER

Emotions often teach us things to help us communicate with other people, but, in fact, a core aspect of our emotions is that they help us to communicate with ourselves. We tend to have strong emotions about things we care about. And when you aren't open to your emotions, you are basically cutting off from yourself the key resource that is actually available to help you to understand yourself better in the world. And a key thing that emotions give us is that emotions help to signal our values.

We grow up in a society that effectively stops a healthy relationship with ourselves and with our emotions, and often what happens is when we feel the emotions, we shut them down or we try to kind of hustle with them. But if we open ourselves up to them, our emotions are a core resource that help us to shape our lives effectively and to deal with a world that is changing, that is complex.

Our social and cultural expectations create almost a tug-of-war within us around our emotions where we're constantly going backward and forward as to whether we should feel something or shouldn't, we're allowed or not allowed, whether it's a good emotion or bad emotion.

[We have to] end the judgment that we have about our emotions. And it's difficult; it's not an easy thing to do, but often there is a level of choice in it: "I am not going to second-guess myself anymore. I am not going to judge myself. This is what I am feeling."

—SUSAN DAVID

INTEGRATE YOUR MIND, BODY, AND SPIRIT

We have to bring girls up to trust their authentic natures and not to deny all parts of themselves. This bifurcation between the head and the heart and between the body and the head has been a catastrophic bifurcation. What we want to encourage girls to do is be whole beings who live in their [bodies], who live in their brains, who live in their hearts, and who understand that compassion is actually not of less value than intellect. And that also the role of girls—and the role of all of us, it seems to me now—has got to be getting out of ourselves, getting out of our single-focused identity to see how we can be of assistance to the greater whole.

—EVE ENSLER

I do believe in body, mind, and spirit—all three are required to act. It is remarkable when the three things come together, whether that's while a person is singing, dancing, climbing, swimming, or surfing. I don't know why it ever got divided. It would be very interesting to know why anybody ever thought they had to define body, mind, and spirit as different, because we are the three. And really feeling alive is those sparks and moments where you have an awareness of all three. When you have a heightened awareness of body, mind, and spirit, it is quite something. By the way, it could be an exhilarating moment or a painful moment, when you have that awareness of all three. When you say that someone broke your heart, it is an awareness of all three.

—ANNA DEAVERE SMITH

8

THE POWER OF BEING AUTHENTIC AND VULNERABLE

Being "insecure at last" means you're actually where you are, you feel what you feel. . . . I think the way to survival is to just honor whatever is inside you, and to keep letting it go through you, as opposed to getting caught in any *one* identity that is false. Part of becoming "insecure at last" is to give up the *need* for "security"—and I'm talking about the idea of a security where you are untouched by change, which, by the way, you're never going to be, because all life *is* change. But were you to give up that impossible idea and focus on freedom, on connection, on compassion, I tell you, it's a glorious life! It's a glorious life. It is *amazing* here in vulnerable land.

—EVE ENSLER

What we all try to do in our lives is amplify our souls—try to be as authentic as we can be and as whole as we can be, regardless of what people think or what society says we should be.

            —JANE FONDA

Be your authentic self. Authenticity is everything. Think of what you have to offer and how unique that is.

           —NANCY PELOSI

I think vulnerability is power. I'm interested in the open-faced sandwiches of the world. I'm less drawn to the people that obfuscate and are withholding and are tricky for no reason. I like vulnerable and open people, and I think when you're that way, you're actually being very brave. By presenting the real truth of yourself, who you really are, you change the molecules in the room.

—AMY POEHLER

9

HOW WE TREAT
ONE ANOTHER

I encourage courtesy—to accept nothing less than courtesy
and to give nothing less than courtesy. If we accept being
talked to any kind of way, then we are telling ourselves we are
not quite worth the best. And if we have the effrontery to talk
to anybody with less than courtesy, we tell ourselves and the
world we are not very intelligent.

—MAYA ANGELOU

Relationships are a classroom for leadership in girls' lives. We
try to give girls the skills to tell their friends how they are feeling, promote their own perspective, negotiate, compromise,
advocate for themselves. There's so much to be gained by just
being able to know and say what you think and feel in your
closest relationships. I feel that that's the point where if you

can do that in your closest relationships, you're developing the ability to do that elsewhere.

In their closest relationships, that's where the mean-girl behavior happens. Some of the female aggression that we see expressed between girls has in common avoiding direct conflict and going behind someone's back, or turning to social media instead of having a direct conversation. That's happening not because girls are inherently cruel, but because society hasn't given them permission to be more direct and no one's really taught them the skills to do it. We have an opportunity to give girls the skills to navigate their conflicts a little bit differently.

If you learn in your closest relationships that what you should do when you get upset is to give someone the silent treatment or roll your eyes, you're going to become a young woman who does the same thing in all areas of your life. It's fine if you want to go on Instagram, but that can't be the only language you speak when you have a problem with someone.

You're not going to wake up one day like Buddha under the tree and just know how to have a difficult conversation with somebody. You've got to learn that. You've got to practice. You've got to try.

—RACHEL SIMMONS

People who disagree with you are not necessarily your enemy. And the truth is that I've met a lot of extreme people who *extremely* disagree with me in very vocal and vociferous ways, and I can still find more I agree with them on than we disagree on. . . .

Even my closest friends, I don't see eye to eye with them on everything. But I have a well-honed habit of focusing on the things we agree on or the ways in which we're alike or the ways in which we're connected.

—SALLY KOHN

We can learn to see ourselves in each other and recognize that human beings are more alike than we are unalike.

—MAYA ANGELOU

I still believe that what we need more than anything now is love—a little bit more acceptance, understanding, forgiveness, listening instead of just talking. I think we need to try a little harder to get inside the hearts and minds of other people.

—DOLLY PARTON

I have a little pillow in my living room that says, "The smile you give is the one you get back," and it really is true, because that's the way we're made. [The human brain] has mirror neurons, which means that if somebody is smiling, you actually feel like smiling. If somebody laughs really hard, you start laughing. If somebody starts crying, you actually can cry. And the mirror neurons are there because by nature we're extremely empathetic. So when you give somebody something, you learn that you get the same feeling back, and that is a win-win for everybody.

—GOLDIE HAWN

⤜10⤛

NINE WAYS TO
HELP YOU OVERCOME
HARD TIMES

1. VIEW YOUR STRUGGLES
AS OPPORTUNITIES TO LEARN

Katharine Hepburn once said to me, "I've learned more from my failures," and it's true: You learn. Somebody else said, "God doesn't look for awards and accolades. God looks for wounds and scars." Most of us are wounded. I would wager that every single person carries wounds. And it's through those wounds that we can blossom.

Don't give up that effort to learn from your wounds and your scars. Understand that the events and the people that gave you those wounds, they had nothing to do with you. It was their problem, and probably *they* had wounds. All we can do is try to take it from here and learn and grow from it. We can't undo the wounds; they're there, and we just let them teach us and let the wounds make us better people.

—JANE FONDA

Some people are born with confidence. Some people are imbued with it based on their circumstance. But for a lot of us, confidence is borne of tragedy and disappointment, and the realization that we can still do more; it's borne of resilience.

—STACEY ABRAMS

It's not failure; it's feedback. You're always getting feedback from whatever experience you have in life, whether it's good or sad or difficult—you keep learning. You've got to keep learning.

—BILLIE JEAN KING

We've all loved and lost, all had a lot of pain, and we're supposed to—we're humans, it's the way it works. But it's how you manage it, how you manage those tears and that pain, how you are able to get yourself out of it.

—GOLDIE HAWN

We may encounter many defeats, but we must not be defeated. It may even be necessary to encounter the defeat, so that we can know who we are. So that we can see, "Oh, that happened, and I rose. I did get knocked down flat in front of the whole world, and I rose. I didn't run away; I rose right where I'd been knocked down." That's how you get to know yourself. You say, "Hmm . . . I can get up! I have so much courage in me that I have the effrontery, the incredible gall to stand up." That's it. That's how you get to know who you are.

—MAYA ANGELOU

I became aware in my own life, when going through difficult times, that you really had a choice in times of crisis to break down and be broken or to break open, which means to let the shock and grief of a hard time open your heart. A door opens, and you have a powerful moment in time to deeply learn from the experience instead of blaming or feeling like a victim. Even if your difficult times come at you out of the blue, even those times open your heart to the magic and power of life, and give you this inner commitment to live every moment.

Because life actually is this mystery and gift. And every moment of it can be full of real radical joy and wakefulness. And for some reason, in our most difficult times we have the best chance to wake up.

—ELIZABETH LESSER

2. EXPRESS YOUR FEELINGS
IN A CREATIVE WAY

Stay strong! There are so many inspirational quotes that I live by, but what also helps me get by every day is writing down my thoughts, experiences, and feelings.

—DEMI LOVATO

I think everybody suffers. Life is filled with suffering of all different types, and you can't escape it—no matter who you are; it doesn't matter. Suffering is an element of life. But if you *do* something with it, like create something, it is a very satisfying way to cope with it.

—MARGARET CHO

My creativity was my voice, and it has proven to be my most important expression. I knew very early on that it was my responsibility to find an outlet for this expression.

—DONNA KARAN

3. STAY POSITIVE

You have to stay optimistic. You do sometimes feel very discouraged, but it's also very important to remain optimistic and to see the silver lining in everything you do. Sometimes things look difficult, like there is no hope, but there is always a small glimmering of silver lining that is in everything.

—WANGARI MAATHAI

What kept me positive? Well, for one, being bitter is exhausting. I've done that. I held it in my shoulders, back, stomach, and face. I aged. I hurt. I cramped. It was no fun. . . . The anger might have kept my body going, but without love, the soul would have just slowly crumbled and burned. It was the love that kept the soul going. So I think to be fully alive, you need both a healthy body and a loving soul.

—LOUNG UNG

You can only be optimistic, because I don't really know how you'd wake up in the morning if you felt pessimistic. It's obviously easy to feel that way with the news—you can watch the news, and it feels like it's the end of the world, very apocalyptic. So I just stay away from the news and try and find people around me who are doing positive things and look to them.

—NATALIE PORTMAN

Everything is going to be fine in the end, and if it's not fine, it's not the end. That's a super bumper sticker—actually, I think I saw it on a refrigerator magnet—but that's like my religion.

—MARGARET CHO

4. PRACTICE GRATITUDE

I have a different outer world because my inner world is one of peace and kindness and consistent grace. I am consistently blessed in my life; literally, goodness and mercy follow me everywhere I go, and that is because I have an attitude of gratitude all the time about my life.

My happiness is in direct proportion to my gratitude. And when I get off track, it's because I have stopped gratitude journaling. It is really the truth that the energy you give to being grateful instantly changes whatever situation you're in if you can figure out something to be grateful for in that moment.

—OPRAH WINFREY

Ms. Winfrey says it best when she says you have to cultivate an attitude of gratitude. I am very grateful for so many things—my breath, my friends, my family, my health, my education, my curiosity, my memories. . . . Even though I went through wars and lost my parents at a very young age, I still have so much to be grateful for.

—LOUNG UNG

5. TAKE TIME FOR STILLNESS
AND REFLECTION

It is amazing how even ten minutes without your cell phone or computer or TV—just you and silence—can wake you up and fill your empty well. Just shutting the door and telling everybody, "Don't bother me for ten little minutes." That's your sacred time to either sit nice and tall, breathe or stretch, or do some physical exercise that awakens the energy inside of you.

—ELIZABETH LESSER

Drowning out the noise of the world helps reconnect you to your own happiness.

—OPRAH WINFREY

You know what happens if you're completely still? Your mind—that little tape that's running "bup, bup, bup," all the noise—it eventually runs off the reel. And you have nothing left to think. All of a sudden, the answers are just there.

—MELISSA ETHERIDGE

Silence is the best way to get real attention, especially from the deep self. In my own case, I know that what I can bring to the world comes from a world of deep silence and quiet. That is where my compass—my moral compass and my internal guide—that's where they live, in that deep quiet.

— ALICE WALKER

6. BREATHE

A conscious focus on breathing helps me introduce pauses into my daily life, brings me back into the moment, and helps me transcend upsets and setbacks. It has also helped me become much more aware of when I hold or constrict my breath, not just when dealing with a problem, but sometimes even when I'm doing something as mundane as putting a key in the door, texting, reading an e-mail, or going over my schedule. When I use my breath to relax the contracted core of my body, I can follow this thread back to my center.

As our breath flows in and out, our tensions gradually give way, as if our breath is massaging us from the inside out, releasing the stresses of the day we're still needlessly holding on to.

—ARIANNA HUFFINGTON

7. REALIZE THAT YOU ARE STRONG

Look what you've already come through! Don't deny it. You've already come through some things that are very painful. You have gone through some pain; it cost you something, and you've come through it. So at least look at that. Have the sense to look at yourself and say, "Well, wait a minute. I'm stronger than I thought I was."

—MAYA ANGELOU

8. HELP YOURSELF BY HELPING OTHERS

What I would say to anyone is, "Stop waiting. Stop retaliating. Stop living your life as if you're going to be rescued, and give what you need the most." Discover your fantasy of what you need the most, what you would want someone to do for you the most, and then go out and give it to someone else. When you give what you need the most, you heal whatever is broken. You will heal, and you will transform whatever pain is inside you. . . . What we are waiting for has always lived inside us.

—EVE ENSLER

I want things to be good because it just kills me when things are not good. And if I wake up in the morning and find there's something going wrong, I try my best to see what I can do to make it better by the end of the day, and I pray hard about it. I work at it. And I just try to keep a good positive attitude. You can't change everything, but you can change some things, and changing some things might change [a situation] enough to where it's bearable or you might do something to lift somebody else's burden. Even when your burdens are too hard to carry, if you try to help somebody with theirs, yours don't seem as bad.

—DOLLY PARTON

9. WHEN YOU'RE READY,
FORGIVE YOURSELF AND OTHERS

A lot of recovering from hardship is how much you blame yourself for making the mistakes you actually made or mistakes that weren't your fault. And women are much harder on themselves than men, so giving women the permission to forgive themselves [is important]. Look, sometimes the mistake or the hardship is not our fault, and sometimes it is, but either way, we are human, and we make mistakes, and recovery depends upon self-compassion. Self-compassion for women in adversity is so important.

—SHERYL SANDBERG

F orgiving is one of the hardest things to do, but it's really necessary. Without forgiving, you don't really move—you can't. It's like this little prison that you're in. And it's so painful, because you feel like you don't deserve to be in prison; it wasn't your fault. And how dare you have to forgive these horrible people. But actually, you do.

—ALICE WALKER

One of the most important gifts you can give to the human race is to forgive people. And mind you, what you do, of course, is you liberate your own self; you liberate yourself from carrying that weight around. When you say, "I forgive you," it's a giant gift—a gift that's first to yourself, because it means you're not toting that burden around and saying, "I have this. I will never forgive you." And then, of course, that means you will never be free, you will never be at ease, you will be continually burdened.

Learning how to forgive is a great lesson to learn. I never had that feeling that I had to carry the weight of somebody's ignorance around with me. And that was true for racists who wanted to use the N-word when talking about me or about my people, or the stupidity of people who really wanted to belittle other folks because they weren't pretty or they weren't rich or they weren't clever. I never had that feeling that I had to carry that around. That was somebody else's problem, not mine.

—MAYA ANGELOU

11

MAKE EACH
MOMENT COUNT

It's a courageous act to just be with whatever is happening at the moment—all of it, the difficult as well as the wonderful.

—EILEEN FISHER

I would say that I've reached a really joyful stage that allows me to be fully present in every moment and to appreciate every person, every encounter, every moment in such a way that I feel so full of life. I'm at that space where there really is no separation between me and life. Where I can literally see the spirit of the divine in every person I encounter.

—OPRAH WINFREY

I enjoy life. I think it's fun. I try to create every moment that I can to just have fun and be with the people that I love and do things that I'm passionate about. And that's my decision to do that. Everybody can do it.

—CAMERON DIAZ

Surfing your life is this idea of finding your center of balance, and then realizing that "nothing gold will stay." The sooner you realize that everything changes—that the things that happen to you are not *you* and that everything will be different all the time and you have such little control over the next wave, then you'll just stay in the moment, find your gravity, and be open to what's coming. Just don't turn your back on the wave—it's coming, no matter what; you can't hide from it. So face the waves, try to catch one, and ride it.

—AMY POEHLER

Every day I have these real small goals—like trying to play the banjo—and that's enough. I think what gives you happiness is every day you just get these little small goals and you accomplish them, and it's awesome.

—MARGARET CHO

In tennis, I take it one ball at a time,

staying in the now, staying in the process.

In every single sport and in life,

being in the moment—when you're in the zone,

when your head and your heart and your gut are

integrated—that's when you do your best.

—BILLIE JEAN KING

Life should be ecstatic; not every minute, but you should definitely have enough ecstasy in your life from time to time to know that you are just completely wired into creation.

—ALICE WALKER

I think that life is a magic carpet ride—it's amazing. Everything about it is mysterious and beautiful and touching and tragic and lovely and mystical. And we waste so much time, almost every minute, swimming against the river. Life is about change; it never stops. And we, as these temporary forms of human beingness, spend most of our time swimming as hard as we can against that river. If we would turn on our back and float on this river, and look up at the sky and around at the banks, it's so beautiful! We don't have to fight it and fight each other. There's enough for everybody, and yet we're greedy and scared. To me, the purpose of life is to enjoy it! It's to enjoy the gift, and to make sure that other people have an opportunity to enjoy the gift.

—ELIZABETH LESSER

We each have this one life gifted to us. I feel that my life is a gift that I want to try to use as wisely as I can. I want to make use of each of these amazing days that come my way to make a bit of difference.

—JANE GOODALL

Every day counts. I believe that every individual counts, and I believe that every day counts, and I try not to waste it. Every day I try to figure out whether there's something I can do that will make a difference.

—MADELEINE ALBRIGHT

⚡12⚡

UNDERSTANDING
FEMINISM

I consider myself a feminist. I mean, I love the definition that it's the whole belief that women are human beings and deserve equal rights, equal access. I think of Elizabeth Cady Stanton, the original women's declaration of rights that [the suffragists] wrote. It was with all the same language but just adding, ". . . and women." Men *and* women. I love feminism; being a feminist is a great thing to be.

—KERRY WASHINGTON

F eminism is my life! It's who I am. For me, it's just a logical way to be. It's the way I approach everything. Feminism to me is like the oxygen we breathe. It's so vitally important to life because women ultimately make life happen. Feminism is really a matter of respect for life and where life comes from and what life is and respect for women's rights and what women want and respect for the earth and, really, respect for the planet—just respect for life itself.

—MARGARET CHO

[My definition of feminism is] to be self-sufficient, to be strong, to be nurturing to friends and family, and to be compassionate. For me, it's kind of being a warrior and fighting through all odds to be an individual—independent and free.

—SANDRA BERNHARD

To me, sometimes when people don't identify themselves as feminists, it's like saying, "I like cars; I think they're great; I use a car every day; it gets me from place to place, but I'm not going to go on record and say that I think cars are good."

That being said, this media discussion about who is and isn't a feminist is yet another example of the media attempting to divide us, to split us apart and have us arguing among each other. I think we need to continue as women to constantly celebrate what we have in common and share, and stop letting this society focus on how we're different—it's really frustrating. The topic of feminism is another example of people co-opting it, taking it out of our hands, and we have to take it back.

—AMY POEHLER

I would say a feminist is somebody who believes

in personal, professional, and political equality.

Period. It doesn't matter if you're a man or a woman

or pink or yellow or whatever. It's those three things.

It's just equality.

— MELISSA ETHERIDGE

* * *

I love Mae West's quote: "Speak up for yourself or you'll end up a rug." I'm a feminist because I'm not going to be walked on. That says it all.

—LOUNG UNG

There are all of these weird societal hurdles and stereotypes that affect women and impact women negatively. And until we get as many women as men into leadership roles, we're not going to problem-solve for a diverse planet.

—SOPHIA BUSH

I care about gender equality because leaving out half of the population will ensure that we don't achieve the kind of results that we really believe in and that we can get to together. At the end of the day, women are powerful; women have a lot to offer.

I was taught to use every single tool that I have in my toolbox to achieve the things that I want. Women are a central part of society; leaving us out means not winning. And if that's the outcome you want, then keep on leaving us out. But if you want to win, if you want to see justice, if you want to experience collective freedom, then women need to be right there at the table with you.

—BRITTANY PACKNETT

I just want every young girl to have a shot at her dream. I have a daughter, and I raised her to believe that she has the power to be whatever she wants to be, but there are a lot of forces that try to tear us all down and tell us we can't achieve whatever we want. It's very personal for me, as a mother of a daughter, and as someone who has seen so many women who have struggled just to get by and who are discriminated against, who are harassed, physically, mentally, sexually. That's not the kind of society I want to belong to. I want to belong to a society that reflects that all lives have dignity and worth that should be valued and treated equally.

—VALERIE JARRETT

Ninety-some years ago, women got the right to vote. When they did, the papers said: "WOMEN GIVEN THE VOTE." Women weren't *given* the right to vote—women *won* that right. They marched, they fought, they starved, and it took decades for women to have the right to vote. What's really important is we have to fight for [gender equality] in that tradition—the rich American tradition of speaking up and standing up for fairness and equality in all aspects of public and private life.

—NANCY PELOSI

Gender equality is critical because right now we live in an unequal society that actually values the lives and the contributions of men over women. And as long as we have a hierarchy of human value in this country, we're actually never going to realize freedom.

—AI-JEN POO

Gender equality has everything to do with trying to build a new foundation that centers on those who have been locked out of history forever. Gender equality is about changing the face of who deserves to get a piece of the pie.

—PATRISSE CULLORS

I think of feminism as the movement to liberate democracy from patriarchy. It's in the interest of men, women, the planet, the future. And it is one of the most important liberation movements in human history.

—CAROL GILLIGAN

There are women who for years have been lying down on the barbed wire for us, who for years have stood up to the ridicule, to the false accusations—and the way is so much clearer and easier now than it's ever been. The world is starting to see that the feminine balance is needed—has to be there and has to be revered—for peace, just for life! We have to have that balance.

We have been in the patriarchy for so long, and it has destroyed everything, and we are in the last throes of it. Young women, now it's your turn. The world is here; we've opened it. Go. Be. Take it. Do not fear. And just speak your truth.

—MELISSA ETHERIDGE

GUYS CAN (AND SHOULD)
BE FEMINISTS, TOO

When women own their strengths, and men own their hearts, that to me is what feminism is—when our full humanity is claimed. You can talk about equal rights, but essentially feminism will come into wholeness when we achieve a social paradigm that allows men and women to become full human beings, rather than women muting themselves and men hardening themselves, which I think is the root of all the problems.

Feminism is for men as well as women; I cannot emphasize that enough. And the only way we are going to make it is if we understand that and speak about it.

—JANE FONDA

Feminism means empowerment. Men can be feminists, too! Many men are feminists. We need feminism. It's not against men; it's about the empowerment of women. It's the respect of women—giving women equal rights, the same opportunities.

—ANNIE LENNOX

Change will come from girls and women and men who understand that for us all to be human beings, instead of being grouped by gender, is good for them, too.

Once men realize that the gender roles are a prison for them, too, then they become really valuable allies. Because they're not just helping someone else, they're freeing themselves. There is a full circle of human qualities we all have a right to, and they're confined to the "masculine" ones, and we're confined to the "feminine" ones. We're missing more, but they're still missing a lot.

—GLORIA STEINEM

I'm the mother of a son in a generation of boys [and] I'm the wife of a man in a generation of men who support strong women, who want their sisters to thrive, who wished their mothers had had greater opportunity and will demand that their daughters have equality. So I have absolutely no doubt that we will never go back and we are moving ahead. And I think it's not just about women rising; it's about men rising, too. I know that sounds counterintuitive, but I think that feminism means supporting men *and* women to create equality that makes our societies better, makes our relationships better, makes our opportunities better.

—ANN CURRY

The more I learned about feminism, the more I realized I'm a feminist because I believe in equality. And I always thought that humanity has two wings, the male and the female, and these wings need to be equivalent in strength in order to fly.

—JUSTIN BALDONI

Every day, we have an opportunity to rebuild our integrity and work toward becoming the men that we are truly capable of being. The road ahead requires us to continually think critically about our own thoughts and behaviors, and to value women enough that we are willing to educate ourselves with the wealth of information that they've put into this world about these issues. The more we lean into the discomfort of challenging ourselves and other men, the easier it becomes. And we are daily faced with opportunities to do so, if only we are willing to open our minds and hearts to create this positive change.

—MATT McGORRY

13

USE YOUR VOICE

I read a study when I was in college about how, in the United States, if you see class president elections, it's like all girls [run], and then in eighth grade no girls run. What happens in there that tells girls to be quiet, be submissive, be meek? It's ridiculous—we're missing out on fifty percent of our potential great people.

—NATALIE PORTMAN

If I've learned one thing in my short life, it's that if you don't tell your story, somebody else is going to tell your story for you.

Doing things that haven't been done before requires us to be uncomfortable. It requires us to speak up when we usually wouldn't speak up. Far too many of us don't want to be uncomfortable. I'm sorry, but if you want to see change, change is uncomfortable! If it was easy, it wouldn't be so hard to get.

—SYMONE D. SANDERS

When you share your values and share your priorities . . . it actually can have a real-world impact, and I want to really inspire women to believe in themselves and to know that their voice, their story, is really important. All women have to find their story and live their story, and all women have to realize that their voice is important.

—KIRSTEN GILLIBRAND

I believe in personal power, and I believe in speaking up— that's where power comes from—and a lot of girls are scared to speak up.

I would say to girls, "Which is more important to you: Is it more important to impress a boy, or is it more important to speak out?" I always encourage my daughter to speak out. Even when she was a kid, she used to have feminist arguments with boys in the class. And I thought, *Good. Good for her.* The boys are not as important as her making her point.

Also, I was always encouraged to talk in my family. They never told me to be quiet. No one ever said, "Be quiet, Joy." And believe me, I must have irritated them plenty. But, I don't know, they just thought I was amusing or something, and they let me just yak it up. So don't tell girls to be quiet. Stop telling us to be quiet; we're not going to be quiet.

—JOY BEHAR

You can't please everybody, so you might as well just speak the truth. That's all your job is: to speak the truth, if nothing else because at least you will know that you were authentic to yourself. At the end of the day, you have to basically answer to yourself, not anybody else. . . . I don't think we can afford to be silent anymore. I think it is expensive to be quiet sometimes. I think it costs us more to be quiet than it does to speak up.

—LUVVIE AJAYI

I always say to girls, you have to be able to speak both languages. If you want to do girl talk and if you want to make everything sound like a question and be like, "OMG, I was kind of, like, going to say that, but I'm not sure. . . ." If you want to talk like that, that's fine. But you also have to learn how to talk like an assertive woman, so that you can use that when it's the right time.

–RACHEL SIMMONS

[Power] is really just about entitling yourself to an opinion. If you can just entitle yourself to giving your opinion, that's the first step, and I think it's the most important one. Often, it's not just with women; minorities and anybody who feels like an outsider tend to silence themselves. It's the invisibility that's the problem. We don't speak up, and we don't feel we have a right to that voice and that opinion. That's where we can really suffer, so I think it's about entitling ourselves to the voice—just having an opinion and voicing it. And that's something that can be taught and that can be encouraged, and the younger, the better. It can happen at any age.

When you feel powerful, you are willing to stand up for your rights; you are willing to stand up for what you believe in, and you are more willing to stand up and be counted.

–MARGARET CHO

[There is] this deep obstacle that many women have, which is a lack of trust in their own voice and a pervading yet unconscious feeling within, bolstered by society, that what they have to say really isn't of value. They're taught as children in the culture at large that women should actually be quiet and demure, that to be feminine is to be more receptive, more quiet, not to be aggressive; [being strong and speaking out] are still thought of as unfeminine qualities. And as long as we think of the feminine as demure and giving over to [someone else], women won't trust their own voice, because to be heard and to be influential, you've got to have a way to sing out with passion and love and self-trust—to sing out your song for everyone to hear. And so women leaders are at a disadvantage, because we are actually taught *not* to sing out with strength and conviction.

—ELIZABETH LESSER

The most important message that I give to young kids and to people I meet across my state, across the country, is that their voices matter. This is a moment in time when we cannot stay silent, when we must speak up. . . . You have to fight back; you have to speak out. You have to do whatever your time and talents will allow you to do to make a difference.

—KIRSTEN GILLIBRAND

I've never really cared about what people thought of me. The only opinions that count are those from my loved ones. I love this quote from Jane Fonda: "You can do one of two things; just shut up, which is something I don't find easy, or learn an awful lot very fast, which is what I tried to do."

Yes, I do put myself out there, but I back it up with research, knowledge, studies, and experience. You're less vulnerable and more powerful if you can defend your points, articulate your thoughts, and be aware of other viewpoints. When I worked with students in high schools, I advised them to learn to argue well and not be afraid of confrontations, not be afraid to disagree. If some guy or teacher is not treating you well, you have a right to speak up! You don't have to lock it away. You don't have to pretend it doesn't hurt. But you have to do it in a way that is powerful. Write it down, practice, rehearse your lines if you need to, but please say something! Because if you don't, twenty years later, you will still be thinking about it: "I should have said this."

—LOUNG UNG

My mother and a lot of other teachers always encouraged original thinking and spirited debate.

—AMY POEHLER

I never would have imagined in the first part of my life that I could have stood up and said anything. . . . What I've discovered is that you can be so much more powerful if you're talking from your soul, from your core self.

—JANE FONDA

Never, ever, ever, ever, ever stop telling the truth. People keep saying that we are in a "post-truth" world. I don't believe that, because the world will only be post-truth if we let it, if *we* stop telling the truth. I don't care what they're saying on TV; I don't care what they're saying in the newspaper. If we know the truth, then it is our responsibility to tell it. And we have no excuse. We have social media at our fingertips; we have outlets like Medium at our fingertips. We have so many opportunities to keep telling the truth.

—BRITTANY PACKNETT

If you can see it, you can be it. But you don't even have to see it at this point. You *are* it. Most importantly, your voice matters. Every voice counts. Every voice matters, and that voice needs to be heard. And by not using your voice, you're doing a disservice not only to yourself but to the community and to the world at large. I like to approach it from, "It's your responsibility, girls. Get over your looks. Get over your insecurities. You have a responsibility to all of us. We need your help."

—JENNIFER SIEBEL NEWSOM

Trust your own outrage. My parents did a really incredible job of making me know that my emotional reactions to the world or to ideas or to other people were valid and valuable. . . . There was respect for the idea that when your gut tells you something is wrong, you trust that—and that it's not just for you. It's for other people who might not be able to speak as loudly or as clearly as you might be able to. Part of your responsibility as a person who cares about people is to trust your own outrage and speak out about it.

—COURTNEY E. MARTIN

It took me quite a long time to develop a voice, and now that I have it, I am not going to be silent.

—MADELEINE ALBRIGHT

Share your voice. We live in a moment where communication is so, so important and so, so accessible. You have something to say, and you should say it. We're all listening.

—DONNA KARAN

14

BE CIVICALLY ENGAGED . . .
AND BE READY TO VOTE

Politics affects all of us. I've met so many people who say, "I don't do politics" or "I don't vote," and it drives me crazy. I say, "Well, see that banana that you're eating? That's political. There was a political decision made behind that banana. And that air you're breathing? That's also political." So we cannot sit back. I spend my time thinking about the young people who don't talk politics at the table because it's taboo. It's not taboo. We need to talk about it everywhere. I want to say to young people, "You might not think about running for district leader or school president or whatever role it is in your town, but you should, because if you don't do it, somebody else will, and they're going to decide how your whole life looks. It's up to you."

—ALESSANDRA BIAGGI

I always have [been] and always will be engaged in the political world. It's something that I've tried to pass on to my own daughter as part of what you need to know in the world.

In addition to math and science and English, know how your government works, know who represents you, and put pressure on them toward the ends and goals that you see as important.

—MELISSA HARRIS-PERRY

* * *

Our government is only going to be as good as the people insist and demand it to be. . . . I encourage everybody to vote if you want to make sure that your priorities, your values, the type of country *you* want the United States to be is well reflected in your elected officials.

Voting is the first step in civic participation. Then you have to get involved in your own community and be a force for good.

—VALERIE JARRETT

People need to vote for a myriad of reasons: because it is a right that, in so many places in the world, people die for; because it is the only way that we actually have a government for the people, by the people. It is the only way to make your voice heard; it is the only way to have any semblance of control over how your life is going to be lived because of how you are governed. Voting is the most important piece of civic duty there is.

—SOPHIA BUSH

People need to vote because a healthy democracy relies upon people actually realizing their right to a voice. It's our way of being able to move toward our dreams and our aspirations for our families, of being able to elect leaders who represent our values and who can actually create the solutions we need in order to live well in this country. There's no choice—we have to vote, and people gave up their lives so that we could. So in many ways it's a responsibility.

—AI-JEN POO

One of the places to make sure that voices like mine and other marginalized voices are heard is at the voting booth. That's not the only thing, but it's definitely a necessary step to make sure that our voices are heard. I often say if our vote didn't matter, people wouldn't be trying to take it away from immigrants and people of color and people living in low-income circumstances. Every single opportunity we have to make our voices heard is something that we have to show up for. And voting is one of those chances.

—BRITTANY PACKNETT

People have to vote because someone died for you to have that right. Someone marched for you, someone sang for you, someone suffered for you to have the right to vote, particularly people of color. That's why we should vote, if nothing else.

We should also vote because it's one of the ways we can harness our power in this country. We live in a democracy that is driven by the vote, and it's driven by the right that we have to choose people to represent us and move our government forward. . . . It's really important for us to understand that voting is a pivotal and important part of the democratic process.

It may feel hopeless sometimes, like "Why should I vote, if my vote doesn't count?" But if you don't vote, it definitely doesn't count.

—TARANA BURKE

Every time I go to the ballot box, I think about those women who gave up their lives (some quite literally losing their lives), went to prison, fought for years and years and years and years so that we would have, as women, the right to participate fully in our country's government. And those women, when they finally got the Nineteenth Amendment, they said the most profound thing: "This is not for ourselves alone." Because in fact, many of them never got to vote under the Nineteenth Amendment they fought to get for you and me and all other women in this country. We have to vote. If we don't vote, we are ignoring history and giving away the future.

—PAT MITCHELL

The voting booth is the only place on earth in which everybody's equal.

—GLORIA STEINEM

15

TAKE CARE OF
THE EARTH

You really can't turn your back on the basics of how you treat each other and how you treat the earth.

—SANDRA BERNHARD

The one important thing that environmentalism does is it shows us and allows us to believe the earth is a living organism. Once we comprehend that, there's no way that we can continue with the destructive behavior that we have [indulged in], because not only is it destructive to us, it's destructive to the earth. And maybe we're not ready to care about ourselves yet, but getting the whole world to think about taking care of the earth is the beginning of taking care of each of our individual selves.

We can still be comfortable, we can still be happy, we don't have to go backward—we just need to go forward in thought. And by waking up tomorrow and saying, "I live in a world that cares about the earth as a living organism, and we care about ourselves," if I just believe that every day, and those around me believe that, then that expands out. And that's where the change comes from—changing the way you think.

—MELISSA ETHERIDGE

I have seen so many beautiful parts of the world, and I'm in awe of it. I'm in awe of nature; it's perfection. When it's working as it's meant to, there's no flaw. And I started seeing the impact of our existence as human beings and the way we utilized the resources. I started seeing that we were flawing that system. We were creating major chaos within it. . . . Everything from deforestation to global warming—what are we doing to this planet? It's our planet. I want to live on a planet that's beautiful and clean and healthy.

We're at a moment where we need to do something. It's time to do something about this, and if we don't do it now, it's going to be too late.

—CAMERON DIAZ

You cannot protect the forests, you cannot protect the land, you cannot protect the environment just by having knowledge alone. You have to take action. And sometimes action means digging a hole, planting a tree, making sure that the trees are protected, making sure that our rivers and lakes are clean. Just having the knowledge doesn't help.

We need action.

— WANGARI MAATHAI

* * *

Life is interconnected. Things that go on in, let's say, the Congo Basin—it may seem incredibly unimportant in the midwestern United States, but when you realize that the loss of the tropical forests in the Congo Basin is having an enormous effect on climate change, and climate change, in turn, is affecting weather patterns all over the world, then you start to realize that life is interconnected. On the other hand, there may be some small ecosystem, and there may be an endangered species—it may be an insect, and so what if it disappears? But maybe that insect is the main prey of a certain kind of bird, and if the insect goes, the bird goes, and maybe that bird was important for dispersing seeds of various plants, and so those plants will start becoming extinct. And one thing leads to another, and none of the biologists know where it's going to stop. The answer to it really is that we know we are all interconnected, and we don't yet know the effects of removing a strand from the web of life.

—JANE GOODALL

The bottom line is that it would serve us well to, first of all, do what an astronaut does. An astronaut learns everything he or she can about their life-support system, and then they do everything they can to take care of it because their life depends on it. We're here hurtling through space on earth with a life-support system—the living ocean, the fabric of life on the land, all of this providing the means of our existence. Protect your life-support system as if everything you care about depends on it, because it does.

—SYLVIA EARLE

I tell the story of a hummingbird that refuses to [flee with] the rest of the animals when a forest is burning and instead decides to go and bring water from the river. The fire is so huge, but with its little beak, it takes a drop of water every time and brings it and puts it on the fire. The moral of the story is that it doesn't matter how small the action is, if we all do what little we can, collectively we can make a difference. There are very many little things that we all can do.

For example, the three R's: reuse, reduce, recycle. And as I say those words, there are so many things individually we can do to reduce—we don't need to consume as much as we are consuming. And we can reuse a lot of things we just throw into the dump and reduce production. The more we reuse, the more we can reduce.

I learned from Japan that you can also try not to waste, especially people who live in very highly industrialized worlds; they are so wasteful. And we waste because there is plenty. This concept in Japan is called *mottainai*; it is a concept that is based in Buddhism, and it is used to encourage the Japanese to be grateful—about what they get from their resources, from their world, from their environment—and to not waste resources, and to be grateful and also to be respectful. Respect,

be grateful, do not waste. I was told that, as the Japanese children would eat rice, if they left even one grain on their plate,
they would be told by their parents, "Oh, what a *mottainai*! You
finish your food!" And it's only one grain of rice.

There is a lot that we as individuals can do. In our homes,
when we go shopping, as we travel, there is so much we can
do. And even though we think that that particular action at an
individual level may be very small, just imagine if it is repeated
several million times. It will make a difference. That hummingbird's actions may look very small, but it is very powerful if it is
repeated many millions of times.

                                        —WANGARI MAATHAI

I just do as much as I can do: be aware of my energy consumption, as far as all the lights in my house, how much power I use,
how much I run the water, set my thermostat, my recycling, my
car. I am trying to retrofit everything as much as possible and
try to do it consciously, as green as possible.

I think people get scared that they're not going to be able
to do it perfectly, that they're going to be criticized. They're
going to be like, "Well, I'm not totally green." Well, you know
what? At this point, we don't care, you know what I mean? Just
a *shade* of green is enough right now. Move a little bit closer
toward this. Because the more people start moving closer and
closer to it, that's something that collectively makes a difference. At this point, all you have to do is to do part of it right and

it will help. If everybody just did one step, collectively it does make a difference.

—CAMERON DIAZ

It is so important for people to understand that, especially this issue of climate change, it really does bring home the fact that we are on one planet, and that some of what human beings do in one corner of the world is going to affect people in a distant corner of the world.

—WANGARI MAATHAI

It's not just climate change; it's the impact of humans as predators on wildlife. . . . We're here because of this great ecosystem—earth, with a miracle ocean and the connections between them, from the tiniest microbes to the largest whale or the tallest tree; it's all connected. You cannot pull it apart without creating a ripple in the system.

Anybody who has a car or rides in a car, anybody who has a computer or uses a computer, just take out one little piece from [that machine]. Sometimes it can keep right on going, doing what it has been doing, more or less. But if you start taking out more pieces, there comes a point when either it stops or it becomes wonky. And we've got a world that's going wonky right now.

—SYLVIA EARLE

People should never give up—there is always hope. Okay, the natural world is in a real crisis situation, but all around the planet, there are extraordinary people who are absolutely determined that certain animal species or plants or ecosystems shall be helped to restore themselves.

—JANE GOODALL

⇃16⇂

YOU HAVE THE POWER
TO ENACT CHANGE

Gandhi was correct: You have to be the change you want to see in the world. And it changes with one person at a time.

—OPRAH WINFREY

Everybody has the power to make changes . . . and every change makes a difference.

—CAMERON DIAZ

[Giving back] changes you in lots of meaningful and profound ways. If [people] choose to get involved, they will be blown away by how joyful it actually is and how much fun it really is. If they put their brains and their energy and their money behind something, they really can contribute to changing the world. And I believe that not just for somebody who's wealthy, but for somebody who volunteers in their local community and gives their time, too. There are a lot of benefits to giving back in either time or resources.

—MELINDA GATES

There's always something to do—always. And the reason that's true is that you always can work with yourself. You don't have to go out and worry about what other people are doing, or how to start this or that out there. You can start ever so much in yourself, and that will evolve outwardly. So just hold that thought—that it really is up to each of us, and we're all trying to get to a place where collectively we can effect change. But we can't really do it being a collective before we are actually self-collected.

—ALICE WALKER

Ordinary people who, like me, are from an extremely humble and, in many ways, troubled background could recognize the need for change and participate with thousands of people around the world and make it happen. I want people to recognize that it's not a special gift given to the rich; it's not a special gift given to men—anybody can participate in transformation. And to me, that means working with people to promote their leadership and ability to be part of transformation. I do a lot of work with young people, and I love it—just helping them understand that they have power and choice and that how they choose what they do can matter a lot in not just their lives, but everybody else's.

—JODY WILLIAMS

Whatever you care about, you can make a difference. You really can. Don't ever underestimate yourself. Do not underestimate the human spirit.

—BILLIE JEAN KING

FIND A CAUSE THAT
RESONATES WITH YOU

The most effective activists are people that are working in an area that resonates from their gut, from their core self—what really matters to them. You have to figure out what that is. And it can be children; it can be your community; it can be green spaces in New York. It can be working with teens. It can be peace; it can be the environment. I mean, there's so much that can be done. And some people can have a big wide swath of influence, and for some people, it can be just a few children. Sometimes all I can do is when I walk down the street—and this matters—is look people in the eye. Acknowledging another person's humanity by something as simple as looking in their eyes is important.

When I go to be with other activists, I feel reborn. You know those things, when you're little, those little hard, crusty things that you drop in water and they kind of bloom into underwater colorful cities almost? I feel like that. I feel like I've been dropped in water, and I'm kind of blooming into color for the first time when I'm with my activist friends. . . . I was raised to feel that service and activism is the rent you pay for life. It's where my lifeblood is. It gives meaning to my life to know that I can be of use.

—JANE FONDA

Explore what you're passionate about, and then have faith that you can make a difference. I always say, a little bit helps. You don't have to become a full-time member of an organization to be effective. A letter helps. As much as you can do helps. You don't have to be perfect; you don't have to be an expert; you don't have to have hours and hours of free time or tons and tons of money. You don't have to go to workshops to know about it. All you have to do is have faith in your passion. And it really makes your life a lot better. You feel that you're making a difference.

—KATHY NAJIMY

VOLUNTEER

I f we all contribute in our own way—even a couple of hours a month of volunteering meaningfully—how awesome would the world be?

—JODY WILLIAMS

D o public service. When young people are asked to help others— through community activity, through cleaning up the neighborhood, through helping at a senior center, through [volunteering] at a local hospital—that opportunity to serve when you are young really creates a heart of service in people. And they understand how important advocacy is and how important service is. If I were to give my young self advice, I would encourage myself to do even more public service and community service.

—KIRSTEN GILLIBRAND

I think volunteering is the most fun thing—it can be really amazing and rewarding and meaningful. I've gotten so much out of it. The coolest thing is the opportunity to meet these people . . . it's inspiring, and it's just incredibly moving to be around them. It completely broadens my view of the world. Sometimes I feel it's more for me. I mean, I'm not really helping them anywhere near as much as they are helping me.

The Internet is the luckiest thing; we have everything at our fingertips right now. You can easily do a search about volunteering locally. The opportunities are all over the place— around your corner or in more exotic locales. But [it's about] everyone finding their own interest.

—NATALIE PORTMAN

My twenty-first birthday was a big milestone for me, but not in the way that our society has conformed to. For my birthday, I wanted to spend my time doing something meaningful and empowering by giving back. I got to work with the Maasai Mamas [in Kenya] in their beading circle, where they hand-make "friend chains." It was such an incredible and exciting experience that I will never forget. For me, getting to work so closely with the people in this culture helped me grow as a person and was one of the most rewarding experiences of my life.

—DEMI LOVATO

There is a great joy and a deep satisfaction in feeling that you are in solidarity with people who are in struggle. And if you can [provide] a service in any way, or if you can lend support or find anything to lift up people in struggle, it feels fantastic!

—EVE ENSLER

STAND UP FOR WHAT YOU BELIEVE IN

It's important to be a voice for the cause that you're fighting for. All of us can use our voices to be as powerful as they can be on any issue that we think is important.

—KIRSTEN GILLIBRAND

[Personal activism] is important. In my Roots & Shoots program, we teach our children a little bit about how to write letters and how to lobby and how to peacefully protest and that sort of thing. I think people should get involved whenever they can, as long as they're not violent. As long as they listen to the opponent, they listen to the other side, and they don't just shout and yell.

—JANE GOODALL

I think that anything's possible to see in our lifetime. I reference this Coretta Scott King line a lot, that freedom is something you have to re-win and re-fight for in every generation. As long as the fight for freedom is a part of everyone's daily form of being, we kind of shift ourselves. . . .

We spend a lot of time trying to have healthy bodies; we eat a salad and work out, and if we binge on something weird, we make up for it the next day. And right now is really a time to be healthy citizens. What does your routine in your life look like—where you're paying attention, where you're signing the petitions, where you're marching, where you're standing up and really using the tools to create a space for solutions?

My friend said the other day that protest isn't the answer— it creates a *space* for the answer, space for the discussion, space to create the balance, to create equality, and to end things like racism and the disparity between the genders. I think that as long as we put that into our routine, then anything can happen in our lifetime.

—CLEO WADE

START SMALL

You know the little saying "Think globally, act locally"? No, act locally first, see that you make a difference, then you dare to think globally.

Start off with your own community; start off with stuff you can do, so that you actually see [the result]. If you're protecting a piece of land near your school from developing, you've learned the difficult part of conservation because you start to realize that saving things isn't always easy, and choices must be made and compromises have to be reached. That's when you learn the reality. And then if children begin to learn that—when they're not too young, like twelve or thirteen—then when they grow up and come into the big, hard world, they already know that you don't give up if it doesn't work the first time; you find another way. That's what's really, really important about it.

—JANE GOODALL

If you think there's nothing you can do to make a difference, get over it. Think about whoever in history has made a difference. How do we have electric lights, how do we have cars, how do we have books, how do we have an alphabet, how do we have numbers? Somebody somewhere at some point discovered these and changed the world.

In the seventies, there was a little girl, a young woman in Texas, who was disgusted by the trash on the beaches, and she started picking up the trash. She didn't ask anybody. She didn't join an organization. She just did what she felt. She just couldn't let it sit there, and she started picking it up, and people around her saw her, and they started picking it up, too.

And then pretty soon it got to be a thing, and an organization called the Center for Marine Conservation, now the Ocean Conservancy, adopted it as a beach cleanup effort. Well, it wasn't just that girl in Texas; around the world, other people, individuals, saw that there was a problem and decided they would do what they could to fix it, one plastic thing at a time. And it has made a difference.

—SYLVIA EARLE

THINK BIG

We need to redefine what we think is normal. Because at one point in time, it was normal in this country for women not to be able to vote; at one point in time in this country, Jim Crow was normal, and it was acceptable. We need to stop talking about what's *normal*, and start thinking about what's *possible*.

—SYMONE D. SANDERS

I have the chance to interact with so many younger women who are so engaged and who have started amazing new ways of being activists. There are so many new ways that young women are actually activating themselves. I'd like to see them thinking bigger. I'd like to see them thinking more systemically, because a lot of those activations are about fighting back against something that's wrong. I think we need to be creating our own agenda for what is right. That needs a different kind of activism. It's harder. It's harder to get that kind of activism going. So I would encourage bigger thinking. But they're brilliant in the use of social media for activism. Think of the things that get changed every day because somebody starts a petition. I think it's fantastic.

—GLORIA FELDT

NEVER LOSE HOPE

Hope is hard. It's painful. It requires patience and it's erratic in its delivery, but it's the most sustainable source of change and improvement possible. So I hold to two ideas: the first is hope, and the second is fight. Both have to be real and true, but they need help, and that means we have to fight for what we want. And I think with those twin obligations—the painful power of hope and the remarkable, sustainable nature of fighting—we can get things done.

—STACEY ABRAMS

If we all give up hope and do nothing, then indeed there is no hope. It will be helped by all of us taking action of some sort. Cumulatively, our small decisions, choices, and actions make a very big difference.

—JANE GOODALL

USE YOUR UNIQUE SKILLS
TO MAKE A DIFFERENCE

Your life is more enhanced when you can take what you've been given and give to others—using the fullest, highest expression of yourself in such a way that it changes not just you but other people.

—OPRAH WINFREY

There are so many things that you can do. Look in the mirror and think about this: You've been commissioned to figure out how you, one person, can make a difference. Take on the responsibility of giving it some thought. Think of one thing, ten things, a hundred things, whatever it is. And then get the information out there. What do you have that is your personal power?

—SYLVIA EARLE

There's so much to do that you will be paralyzed if you sit around thinking, "What's the best thing I can do? Or the most effective? Or who's the neediest?" These are questions that actually don't serve us. What serves us is to just pay attention to where we really feel called. I think it's less about figuring out what's the best thing to do or who's the most needy; it's really about who you are—what are the resources you bring, and how can you match that with what the world needs?

—COURTNEY E. MARTIN

My advice would be to take the tools and the skills and the resources of every kind that you have and go out, find something that you know is not fair, is not just, and begin to change it. In whatever way you know, in whatever way is appropriate for you—but don't ignore it. Don't think it's somebody else's job to change it. Confront it in your own way, and make it your job to make change.

—ANITA HILL

SHOW COMPASSION TO OTHERS

The principle of caring is an extraordinarily deep value.

—EVE ENSLER

For me, nothing is more rewarding than helping others who are struggling.

—DEMI LOVATO

Trying to grow empathy within yourself is revolutionary. It doesn't have to be some huge thing. It can be trying to be the best person you can be and having empathy and taking it from there.

Empathy means you can put yourself in someone else's shoes, and the step beyond empathy is compassion. That puts empathy into action. The ultimate thing is to have compassion. You take your empathy for other human beings and turn it into active compassion, so that you want to join with them and do something about it. . . . It is important to really connect with people and listen to them and understand our common goals and suffering and joy. Our common humanity—we have to keep reminding ourselves of that. And not being afraid of "other," of people who aren't like us.

—JANE FONDA

We can make a lot of organic change by listening as much as we speak (if we have more power than the people we're with) and speaking as much as we listen (if we have less power than the people we're with).

—GLORIA STEINEM

There are so many people who have interacted with some attempt at social change. Just being outside of yourself . . . you care about something other than you. Just to have something that feels like, "Oh, this is a human connection," that means something. It makes you feel good.

—AMY POEHLER

Giving, loving, caring, empathy and compassion,

going beyond ourselves and stepping out of our

comfort zones to help serve others—this is the only

viable answer to the multitude of problems the

world is facing.

— ARIANNA HUFFINGTON

* * *

All we can do is to love each other. I just live that every moment, every second.

—MELISSA ETHERIDGE

Love others: The only way to accomplish and realize the love and peace we each want is to share it with one another throughout the world.

—DONNA KARAN

17

BELIEVE IN YOUR DREAMS AND PURSUE YOUR PASSIONS

Girls need to be reminded that the sky's the limit and everything they want to do is possible.

—AMY POEHLER

We all have the ability to do whatever we set out to do. You just find the ways; you create the opportunities. If you just follow your heart . . . you can do anything.

—CAMERON DIAZ

I think with these young girls these days . . . they have to have the confidence that they can do anything and can just reach for the stars. Go for it! Swing for the fences! They may end up someplace between here and the fences, but they'll end up a long way down the road. So I say: Know your power, respect what is inside of you and value it, and be ready for the opportunity that comes along.

—NANCY PELOSI

Be open to opportunities. See the opportunities when they appear, and seize them. . . . Women need to follow their hearts and their minds and not conform to social pressures. And I think we also need to be acutely aware of opportunities when they arise and seize them with both hands.

—ANA NAVARRO

If you're just willing to hang in there and be tough and follow your dreams with commitment and courage, you can do anything.

—KAY BAILEY HUTCHISON

EIGHT WAYS TO ACHIEVE YOUR DREAMS

1. DON'T LET FEAR OF FAILURE HOLD YOU BACK

I always go back to my grandmother's advice to me the first time I fell and hurt myself. She said to me, "Honey, at least falling on your face is a forward movement." And that came back to me many times as I failed to get the job or failed to do things perfectly or whatever. You have to be willing to be brave enough to risk falling on your face, to risk failing. Everything we do is about taking risks.

—PAT MITCHELL

Making mistakes and failing isn't fatal. It's painful, but it's not fatal as long as we're willing to learn from it and we don't allow those mistakes to temper our willingness to return to ambition. We still have to try.

—STACEY ABRAMS

Don't worry about falling down or failing or stumbling. When you do that, write down what the experience was, why you did it, how you did it, and get your butt back up. Don't stay down.

—DONNA BRAZILE

2. BE WILLING TO TAKE RISKS

Here's one thing that I worry about: I worry that girls in particular, and just in general, we're not willing to make mistakes. We're very nervous about making a wrong move, and we worry that if we make the wrong move, then the consequences will mean that we never recover from them. It's okay—in fact, it's better than okay—to make mistakes, really big mistakes sometimes. So I would want to say to young women, "Hey, run for office, even if you think you're going to lose. Take a hard class, even if you're going to get a C in it. Go ahead and follow love, even if it doesn't work out." We need just a little bit of courage to make mistakes, because that strikes me as where all the good stuff happens.

—MELISSA HARRIS-PERRY

The message my parents taught me that has contributed most to my ability to create change in the world is this: If you want something and you've never had it before, you're going to have to do something you've never done before in order to get it.

—TIFFANY DUFU

3. BE BRAVE

Being brave is not being unafraid but feeling the fear and doing it anyway. When you feel fear, try using it as a signal that something really important is about to happen.

—GLORIA STEINEM

What drives me? There's something in me that at those junctures in my life where I've had the opportunity to take on a greater responsibility, I've just decided I was going to muster up the courage and give it my best shot. And where did that come from? Some of it is the strength that comes from those that support you and believe in you, and your family is certainly an important piece of that, but ultimately it has to come from your own heart, where you have a sense that you want to do it and you're going to muster up all the courage you have and just go for it. And I'm always amazed that once I get to that point in my own heart, how then others come along and are helpful. But if you're waffling, then the others aren't as confident to support you. You have to show that confidence in yourself to begin with. Don't hold back. The sky's the limit. And just be bold. Be bold.

—CATHY McMORRIS RODGERS

There is no one way to [find the courage to face your fear]. I think it just comes from acknowledging the fact that it is scary, but then taking a deep breath, swallowing hard, and just doing whatever that is anyway. There is no easy way—just do it.

—LUVVIE AJAYI

4. DON'T LISTEN TO NAYSAYERS

One of the most important things I've learned is that, as soon as you realize the thing that you want to go for, you're going to be met with resistance. As soon as I decided to run for office, I was told no probably more times than I have ever been told no in my life. I was told, "No, it's not your turn," which is something women hear a lot. I just said, "I *am* doing this. I'm going to take my turn. I'm not going to wait for somebody to anoint me or choose me. I have got to step up." I saw a problem in my community, and I wanted to fix it by running for office.

—ALESSANDRA BIAGGI

Don't let people tell you what you can't do. If it's something that you really want to do, you're going to have to have the fortitude to just know, even when there are naysayers, that you're not going to listen to them.

—KELLY AYOTTE

5. USE YOUR TALENTS AND GIFTS

You are a whole citizen bringing yourself—the gifts you have to offer—to the world.

—OPRAH WINFREY

It is really about being an individual. It's about really tapping into your source as a person, as a human being. Why do you think you're here? What do you want to say? What do you want to accomplish through this journey? Whatever you do—whether you are a lawyer or a chef or a street cleaner—what is your message to yourself, and what is your message to the universe?

—SANDRA BERNHARD

6. DON'T GIVE UP

My advice to anyone who cares about something is to just not give up. Don't be afraid to fail. Keep fighting. Every time you move the ball forward, you can build on that success.

One thing my grandmother always told me is that I could do anything I wanted as long as I didn't give up and just worked hard at it every day. There is nothing that you cannot do if you put your mind to it and really fight hard.

—KIRSTEN GILLIBRAND

I had a father who told me the great thing about life is that you could always change, and so I never felt boxed in. I never felt that I had to continue to do what I was doing, so I took other leaps. I took a lot of risks. And I would say the advice that I would offer to anybody is to follow your passion and then take the high road. Be sure that, whatever you do, you can get up and look at yourself in the morning and be happy about it.

—MARTHA NELSON

At a certain point in life, you have to do what you think is right and just keep marching until someone pays attention.

—MARIA SHRIVER

7. STRIVE TO REACH YOUR FULL POTENTIAL

You want happiness and joy for yourself. You want to be able to live a life that fulfills the truest, highest expression of who you know yourself to be. That is what makes you feel whole, and that is what makes you feel complete. This common bond that we all share is that we're all looking for the same thing.

—OPRAH WINFREY

I am always aiming toward heaven on earth, which I believe is the promise that we all feel in our hearts could be possible. If we didn't think it was possible, we wouldn't continue to dream of it, look for it, create it in our families and in our workplaces. I think that flame is in every human being—to aim for the best in the human spirit. And I will, forever, as long as I'm alive, believe that and work for that. And it's contagious. To be positive and optimistic and try to make your life a model of something beautiful is contagious. And I want to teach people to have that faith and positivity so they can be contagious forces in the world also.

—ELIZABETH LESSER

I've been undergoing a great personal and spiritual transformation. I realized that I had to tear my whole old life down and build it the way that I want it, the way that *I* want my life to be.

—INDIA.ARIE

What do you want to do and be? There's a world of possibility out there, not just in terms of jobs, but in terms of the kind of life you want to lead. You can do anything. I think people need to actually live that.

—SOLEDAD O'BRIEN

8. BE DARING

We should have aggressive and wild ambitions that are only anchored by plans, not by doubts. . . . Do not edit your desire. We are entitled to ambition. We are entitled to success. We are entitled to failure. And any moment of compromise on those three things starts to weaken who we are. I remember when I mentioned in a *Cosmo* article that I wanted to be president of the United States one day, and just the screams that came at me, particularly from men: "How dare [you] speak aloud such a dramatic ambition?" And my response was, "Of course I should. If I don't say it out loud, how will others say it to themselves?"

The minute we allow ourselves to be silenced and to be told that what we want is too much, then we're beginning to weaken who we are and what we can be. I especially want young women to understand that we are capable of everything.

—STACEY ABRAMS

How powerful are we that we are able to walk away from so many things, toward many things—the power of having our own two feet to take us places? Move your feet in the directions you want your life to go. When you have an inkling, summon your courage, let your heart beat wildly, let it go, and see where it takes you. Then take that first step.

—LOUNG UNG

Right now is the time when we need dreamers. Right now is the time when we need people who are willing to imagine. I don't know where we would be if Dr. King hadn't been willing to dream. I don't know where we would be if Harriet Tubman didn't actually think, "No, we can be free no matter what everything in life is telling us." I don't know where we would be if Cesar Chavez hadn't said, "We actually can have equity for people who are working and tilling our land." I don't know where we would be if Rosa Parks hadn't dared to actually sit in that seat on that bus. We need people with daring.

—BRITTANY PACKNETT

18

WISHES FOR THE FUTURE

[My wish for the future is] a world where girls are valued, because they must be. They have so much to contribute. And then a world where a woman's voice really makes a difference, because [women] have a different set of values, and if we speak them and live them, then the world will reflect that. And that's bound to be a more equitable and just place.

—PAT MITCHELL

I wish that we could look into each other's faces, into each other's eyes, and see our own selves. I hope that the children have not been so scarred by their upbringing that they only think fear when they see someone else who looks separate from them.

—MAYA ANGELOU

We already have the material means to eradicate deep poverty and thereby eradicate hunger. We have the material means to begin the tremendous cleanup of the environmental messes we've created. We have, I believe, the psychological, emotional, and spiritual means to create a world without war. We have the material means to create a world in which unnecessary human suffering has been drastically diminished. My vision for the future is that we do those things. And I think we will.

—MARIANNE WILLIAMSON

[My wish for the children of the future is] that they are able to live in a clean, peaceful world. I have always believed that we are on an upward trajectory and that everything is for the best in this best of all possible worlds.

—MADELEINE ALBRIGHT

I just hope that [girls] find a new revolution, and that revolution will be beauty—that they feel beautiful and feel how precious they are. [When I was young,] I wish somebody had told me how beautiful I was and really, really tried to make me understand that. So whenever I see young people, I always try to make them really understand how beautiful they are and how exciting everything is and how great their lives are going to be and how feeling beautiful will help them, if they could get that into their head. I just want to make sure they have *that*.

—MARGARET CHO

[I wish for] clarity and the desire for the truth and to be free from fear. To create and move this humanity to the great places that it can get to.

—MELISSA ETHERIDGE

[My wish is] that basically we come to our senses! That we really, truly do start regaining wisdom. If we just regain wisdom, and join our hearts to our heads, then I think in the future we would not be making the decisions that some of these big multinational corporations are making. We wouldn't decide to throw pesticides over huge areas of the land knowing it's actually going to harm not only the pests but also biodiversity and, eventually, us. We wouldn't be building nuclear plants not knowing what to do with the nuclear waste—all of these decisions affect the future. My hope for the future is that we learn wisdom again.

—JANE GOODALL

Dear God, let me be the change I want to see.

—ANNIE LENNOX

[My wish is that all girls know] that they have a right to be here, that they have a right to their voice, that they have a right to their emotions, that they have a right to their power, that they have a right to their dreams, and that they have a right to their bodies—whatever shape and size they are—and whatever they desire. And that girls can walk anywhere they want and feel safe wherever they are and know from the minute they're born that they were chosen . . . that everybody wants them here.

—EVE ENSLER

sometimes it's just a matter of touching that place that can be opened to the reality that we can do so much more than we think we can. My deepest desire is for people and the world to be happy. I will always believe this is possible and seek to learn how I can contribute.

—ALICE WALKER

I love the Buddhist prayer "May all beings everywhere be happy and free." The second line is "And may my practice of yoga contribute to that happiness and that freedom." For me, by saying "yoga," it's not the poses alone—because I really don't practice my yoga as much anymore—but may my practices in life, may my behaviors contribute to that happiness and that freedom. I think that's it: May all beings everywhere be happy and free.

—KERRY WASHINGTON

Young people might be encouraged to know that, in some respects, they are the teachers and we—parents and grandparents like me—are the ones who need to learn something. Today's youth have developed extraordinary tools for communicating, for gathering information, and for organizing to get things done. I hope they will become effective citizens and leaders by using these tools to make their communities, their countries, and this world a better place.

—SANDRA DAY O'CONNOR

My wish for the future is for all children to have sustenance and peace and a healthy planet and respect for themselves and for everybody around them—to really have a wonderful, fulfilled life.

—SANDRA BERNHARD

[The message I would most want to instill in a child is] that they have the choice to be the best they can be, that they have the power, and that they themselves matter. Because children, I believe, don't feel that they have much of an imprint—and they *are* our imprint. They are our future; they are going to inherit this world. And I want them to feel that they can do it.

—GOLDIE HAWN

⇒ BIOGRAPHIES ⇐

Stacey Abrams is an author, serial entrepreneur, nonprofit CEO, and political leader. After eleven years in the Georgia House of Representatives—seven as minority leader—Abrams became the 2018 Democratic nominee for governor of Georgia, where she won more votes than any other Democrat in the state's history. She has founded multiple organizations devoted to voting rights, training and hiring young people of color, and tackling social issues at both the state and national levels, including Fair Count and Fair Fight Action. She is the author of *Lead from the Outside: How to Build Your Future and Make Real Change.*

Luvvie Ajayi is a bestselling author, speaker, digital strategist, and veteran blogger. She is executive director and cofounder of the Red Pump Project, a national nonprofit that educates women and girls of color about HIV/AIDS. She is also the author of the *New York Times* bestseller *I'm Judging You: The Do-Better Manual.*

Madeleine Albright, PhD, served as US ambassador to the United Nations and went on to become the first woman to hold the position of US secretary of state. She is a professor at Georgetown University and the author of several bestselling books.

Dr. Maya Angelou (1928–2014) was an accomplished poet, award-winning writer, performer, dancer, actress, director, and teacher. She was also an activist for social causes and civil rights, which included organizing with Dr. Martin Luther King Jr., marching for women's rights with Gloria Steinem, and lobbying on behalf of marriage equality.

India.Arie is an R&B singer-songwriter, producer, and philanthropist. She has received four Grammy Awards and twenty-one Grammy nominations, and has sold ten million albums worldwide. In 2008, she launched her own music label, Soul-Bird Music. She has also worked steadily throughout her career to champion causes close to her heart. She has traveled to Africa numerous times to address the AIDS crisis.

Kelly Ayotte served as US senator for New Hampshire from 2011 to 2017. Prior to her time in office, she was a longtime prosecutor and New Hampshire's first female attorney general. She now serves on the board of directors of Winning for Women.

Justin Baldoni is an actor, producer, director, and social entrepreneur focused on creating and effecting positive change. He is cochairman and cofounder of Wayfarer Entertainment, an award-winning media studio focused on good social storytelling content. He also created the roundtable-style talk show *Man Enough*, which invites all men to challenge the unwritten rules of traditional masculinity. He is best known for playing Rafael Solano on the award-winning TV series *Jane the Virgin.*

Joy Behar is a comedian, writer, actor, and cohost of *The View.* She has hosted several of her own TV shows, including *The Joy Behar Show* and *Joy Behar: Say Anything!* She is the author of a number of books, including *When You Need a Lift: But Don't Want to Eat Chocolate, Pay a Shrink, or Drink a Bottle of Gin* and, most recently, *The Great Gasbag: An A-to-Z Study Guide to Surviving Trump World.*

Sandra Bernhard is a comedian, performer, actress, singer, author, and activist. She is the host of the hugely popular *Sandyland*, her daily radio show on SiriusXM's Radio Andy channel 102, for which she won a Gracie Award.

Alessandra Biaggi is a Democratic state senator representing New York's Thirty-Fourth District since January 2019. During the historic 2016 election, she was the deputy national operations director for Hillary Clinton's presidential campaign.

Carol Moseley Braun served as Democratic US senator for Illinois from 1993 to 1999 and was the first African American woman to be elected to the US Senate. In 2003, she campaigned for the Democratic presidential nomination. She is also a civil rights and women's rights activist.

Donna Brazile is a veteran Democratic political strategist and activist, adjunct professor, author, syndicated columnist, political commentator, and vice chair of voter registration and participation at the Democratic National Committee.

Tarana Burke is a civil rights activist who was the original founder of the #MeToo movement, which she started in 2006. In 2017, the movement blossomed into a worldwide campaign to raise awareness about sexual harassment, abuse, and assault.

Julie Burton is president of the Women's Media Center, a feminist organization that works to make women visible and powerful in media and society. For more than a decade, Burton was on the front lines of the women's movement as the youngest CEO of a national pro-choice political action committee, Voters for Choice, where she is now executive director. She is also the founding director of URGE/Choice USA, PFAW Women's Council, and Project Kid Smart.

Sophia Bush is an actress, activist, director, and producer. She starred as Brooke Davis in the WB/CW drama series *One Tree*

Hill. From 2014 to 2017, she starred in the NBC police procedural drama series *Chicago P.D.* She is an advocate for women's rights and LGBTQ rights, and encourages people to be politically engaged and vote.

Margaret Cho is a stand-up comedian, actress, bestselling author, activist, singer, and blogger. She has won numerous awards for her efforts to promote equal rights for all people, regardless of race, sexual orientation, or gender identity.

Katie Couric is an award-winning journalist, producer, *New York Times* bestselling author, cancer advocate, podcast host, and documentary filmmaker. She was coanchor of the *Today* show on NBC for fifteen years before going to CBS and becoming the first woman anchor of a nightly news broadcast. She is the founder and head of Katie Couric Media.

Patrisse Cullors is an artist, activist, organizer, educator, and popular public speaker. She is cofounder of the Black Lives Matter Global Network and founder and board chair of the grassroots Los Angeles–based organization Dignity and Power Now. She has been on the front lines of criminal justice reform for the last twenty years. In 2016, she coauthored the bestselling memoir *When They Call You a Terrorist: A Black Lives Matter Memoir.*

Ann Curry is a former NBC News national and international correspondent and former cohost of the *Today* show. She is the head of her own production company, Ann Curry, Inc., through which she recently produced the PBS series *We'll Meet Again*. The winner of seven national news Emmy awards and the recipient of numerous humanitarian awards, she has been recognized for her coverage of global conflicts, nuclear tensions, and humanitarian crises, and for groundbreaking journalism on climate change.

Susan David, PhD, is an award-winning psychologist on the faculty of Harvard Medical School, the cofounder and codirector of the Institute of Coaching at McLean Hospital, CEO of Evidence Based Psychology, an in-demand speaker and consultant, and author of the bestselling book *Emotional Agility*.

Cameron Diaz is a former model who became one of the most sought-after and highest-paid actresses. She has starred in numerous films, including *The Mask*, *Charlie's Angels*, *There's Something About Mary*, *Bad Teacher*, and many others. She is also a devoted environmentalist and the coauthor of the *New York Times* bestsellers *The Body Book* and *The Longevity Book*.

Tiffany Dufu is a catalyst-at-large in the world of women's leadership and the author of *Drop the Ball: Achieving More by Doing Less*, a memoir and manifesto that shows women how to cultivate the single skill they really need in order to thrive: the ability to let go. She is also founder and CEO of The Cru, a peer coaching platform for women looking to accelerate their professional and personal growth.

Dr. Sylvia Earle is a legendary oceanographer, explorer, author, and lecturer. She has been a National Geographic Society explorer-in-residence since 1998 and is the founder, president, and chairman of Mission Blue: The Sylvia Earle Alliance, which inspires action to explore and protect the ocean. She is also the director for several corporate and nonprofit organizations.

Eve Ensler is an internationally acclaimed Tony Award–winning playwright, performer, and activist, as well as the author of *The Vagina Monologues*. She is the founder and artistic director of V-Day, the global movement to end violence against women and girls. She is the author of several books, including *I Am an Emotional Creature*, *In the Body of the World*, and, most recently, *The Apology*.

Melissa Etheridge is one of rock music's great female icons, as well as a human rights activist. She is a two-time Grammy winner, multiplatinum recording artist, and 2007 Oscar winner for Best Original Song for "I Need to Wake Up," which she wrote for the documentary *An Inconvenient Truth*.

Gloria Feldt is the cofounder and president of Take the Lead, whose mission is to bring women to parity in leadership positions across all sectors of work and civic life by 2025. She is the former president and CEO of Planned Parenthood and the bestselling author of *No Excuses: 9 Ways Women Can Change How We Think About Power*. She teaches a course on women, power, and leadership at Arizona State University.

Eileen Fisher is a fashion designer and the founder and chairwoman of EILEEN FISHER, Inc., which she began in 1984 with $350 in her bank account and not knowing how to sew. Now, thirty-five years later, EILEEN FISHER has stores across the United States, the United Kingdom, and Canada. The Eileen Fisher Foundation and the Eileen Fisher Community Foundation support programs for women and girls worldwide. She is the cocreator of the Eileen Fisher Leadership Institute, a nonprofit that supports leadership in young women through self-empowerment, connection with others, and activism in their communities.

Jane Fonda is an Academy Award–winning actress, a bestselling author, and an activist and advocate for environmental issues, human rights, and the empowerment of women and girls. She is a cofounder of the Women's Media Center, which works to make women and girls more visible and powerful in media. Fonda also stars in Netflix's hit series *Grace and Frankie*.

Melinda Gates is a philanthropist, businesswoman, and global advocate for women and girls. She is cochair of the Bill & Melinda Gates Foundation, the largest private foundation in the world. She is the author of *The Moment of Lift: How Empowering Women Changes the World.*

Kirsten Gillibrand is a Democratic US senator representing New York. After first being elected to the House of Representatives in 2006, Kirsten Gillibrand was appointed to serve in the Senate seat vacated by Hillary Clinton in January 2009. She won reelection in 2018 with 67 percent of the vote. She is the founder of the Off the Sidelines initiative to get more women civically engaged and is the author of *Off the Sidelines* and *Bold & Brave.* In 2019, she announced her run for president in 2020.

Carol Gilligan, PhD, is a writer, activist, professor at New York University, and the author of the landmark book *In a Different Voice*, which transformed psychological theory and feminist thinking. As a member of the Harvard faculty for more than thirty years, she held the university's first chair in gender studies. In 1996, she was named by *Time* magazine as one of the twenty-five most influential people. With her graduate students at NYU, she founded the Radical Listening Project. Her latest book, coauthored with Naomi Snider, is *Why Does Patriarchy Persist?*

Dr. Jane Goodall is a world-renowned primatologist, speaker, and author. She founded the Jane Goodall Institute, a global wildlife and environment conservation organization, as well as Roots & Shoots, a global nonprofit that empowers young people to make a positive difference for all living things.

Melissa Harris-Perry is the Maya Angelou Presidential Chair Professor at Wake Forest University and the founding director of the Anna Julia Cooper Center. She is also the former host of MSNBC's program *Melissa Harris-Perry*, an award-winning author, the founder and codirector of the innovative bipartisan program Wake the Vote, editor at large for ELLE.com, and cofounder of Perry Political Partnership, a political consulting business.

Goldie Hawn is an Academy Award–winning actress and founder of the Hawn Foundation, a charity whose signature program, MindUP, helps children develop the mental fitness necessary to thrive in school and throughout their lives. She is the author of *10 Mindful Minutes.*

Dr. Caroline Heldman is a professor of politics at Occidental College in Los Angeles with a research specialization in media, the presidency, and systems of power (race, class, and gender). She is also the executive director of the Representation Project, which inspires individuals and communities to challenge limiting gender stereotypes and to shift norms. She has published numerous articles and six books.

Anita Hill is an attorney, professor at Brandeis University, and chair of the Hollywood entertainment industry's Commission on Eliminating Sexual Harassment and Advancing Equality. In 1991, her testimony about sexual harassment at the Senate confirmation hearings of Clarence Thomas gave her national exposure. She is the author of *Reimagining Equality: Stories of Gender, Race, and Finding Home* and her autobiography, *Speaking Truth to Power.*

Arianna Huffington is the founder, former president, and former editor in chief of the *Huffington Post.* She is the founder and CEO of Thrive Global, an organization that helps individuals, companies, and communities improve their well-being and performance and unlock their greatest potential. She is the author of fifteen books, including *Thrive: The Third Metric to Redefining Success and Creating a Life of Well-Being, Wisdom, and Wonder* and *The Sleep Revolution: Transforming Your Life, One Night at a Time.*

Kay Bailey Hutchison is the US ambassador to NATO and was the first woman elected to represent Texas in the US Senate, which she did from 1993 to 2013, as a member of the Republican Party. She is also a bestselling author of three books: *Unflinching Courage: Pioneering Women Who Shaped Texas*; *American Heroines: The Spirited Women Who Shaped Our Country*; and *Leading Ladies: American Trailblazers.*

Valerie Jarrett is a businesswoman, lawyer, and advocate for equity and justice. She was senior advisor to President Barack Obama during his eight years in office. She is the author of *Finding My Voice: My Journey to the West Wing and the Path Forward.*

Donna Karan is a renowned fashion designer and philanthropist who launched Donna Karan New York, DKNY, and, most recently, Urban Zen, a lifestyle brand and foundation that addresses wellness, education, and the preservation of culture through artisan communities. She is the author of *My Journey*, her memoir.

Billie Jean King is a tennis legend, winning thirty-nine Grand Slam titles, including a record twenty titles at Wimbledon and defeating male opponent Bobby Riggs in the "Battle of the Sexes" match. She is also a longtime champion of social justice, gender justice, and equality. In 1974, King founded the Women's Sports Foundation, a powerful organization dedicated to ensuring that all girls have equal access to sports. In 2014, she established the Billie Jean King Leadership Initiative, aimed at achieving diverse, inclusive leadership in the workforce.

Sally Kohn is a political commentator and columnist who frequently appears on CNN, MSNBC, and Fox News. She is the author of *The Opposite of Hate: A Field Guide to Repairing Our Humanity* and is the host of the podcast *State of Resistance*. Her three TED Talks have been viewed more than four million times.

Barbara Lee is a Democratic US representative serving the people of California's Thirteenth Congressional District since 1998. She has long advocated for legislative action to end poverty, as well as for ending HIV and ensuring an AIDS-free generation.

Annie Lennox is a singer-songwriter, campaigner, and activist. She has sold more than eighty million records and has won countless awards, including four Grammys, a Golden Globe, and an Academy Award. She is the founder of SING, a humanitarian organization that raises awareness for the HIV/AIDS pandemic in Africa.

Elizabeth Lesser is the cofounder and senior advisor of Omega Institute, the largest adult education center in the US focusing on health, wellness, spirituality, social change, and creativity. She is the cofounder of the Omega Women's Leadership Center, which grew out of the popular Women & Power conference series featuring women leaders, activists, authors, and artists from around the world. She is also a bestselling author whose books include *The Seeker's Guide*, *Broken Open*, and *Marrow*.

Demi Lovato is a Grammy-nominated and multiplatinum-selling singer, songwriter, actress, advocate, philanthropist, and businesswoman. She is a global advocate for LGBTQ and mental health, as well as an outspoken advocate for young people everywhere. She is the recipient of GLAAD's Vanguard Award and the author of *Staying Strong: 365 Days a Year*.

Wangari Maathai (1940–2011) was the first African woman to win the Nobel Peace Prize. She founded the Green Belt Movement, a nonprofit organization that has planted more than fifty-one million trees across Kenya. She also cofounded the Nobel Women's Initiative and authored four books.

Courtney E. Martin is a blogger, speaker, and facilitator, and the author/editor of five books. She writes frequently for the *New York Times* and *BRIGHT Magazine*, among other publications. Courtney is also the cofounder of the Solutions Journalism Network and FRESH Speakers, Inc., and has consulted with a wide variety of organizations—such as TED, the Aspen Institute, the Obama Foundation, and the Sundance Institute—on how to make impactful, story-rich social change.

Matt McGorry is an actor, producer, activist, and self-described intersectional feminist. He is best known for his roles as Asher Millstone in Shonda Rhimes's hit ABC drama *How to Get Away with Murder* and John Bennet on the Netflix original series *Orange Is the New Black*. He is an ambassador for the Representation Project, which inspires individuals and communities to challenge limiting gender stereotypes and to shift norms.

Pat Mitchell is a groundbreaking media icon, Emmy Award–winning and Academy Award–nominated producer, global advocate for women's rights, and cofounder, curator, and editorial director of TEDWomen. She was formerly the president and CEO of PBS and was the first woman to hold that position. Mitchell also served as president and CEO of the Paley Center for Media and president of CNN Productions. She is the author of *Becoming a Dangerous Woman: Embracing Risk to Change the World.*

Robin Morgan is an award-winning poet, novelist, journalist, activist, and bestselling author. She is the former editor in chief of *Ms.* magazine, founder of the Sisterhood Is Global Institute, and cofounder (with Jane Fonda and Gloria Steinem) of the Women's Media Center. She currently writes and hosts *WMC Live with Robin Morgan*, a syndicated weekly radio program with a national and international audience in 110 countries around the world.

Kathy Najimy is an actor, director, writer, producer, and activist known for her memorable performances in more than twenty-five films and one hundred television projects. As a proud feminist and social justice advocate, she has been recognized with numerous honors for her enthusiastic work supporting women's, girls', and LGBTQ rights; AIDS awareness and prevention; animal rights; and reproductive rights. She frequently travels the country as a keynote speaker on these issues.

Ana Navarro is a Republican strategist, CNN political commentator, Telemundo contributor, and cohost of *The View*. She was the national Hispanic campaign chairwoman for John McCain in 2008 and national Hispanic cochair for Jon Huntsman Jr.'s 2012 campaign.

Martha Nelson is the global editor in chief of Yahoo. She was the founding editor of *InStyle* magazine, and she was the first female editor in chief of Time Inc., where she oversaw the editorial content for the media company's twenty-one brands. She is a trustee of both the National Trust for Historic Preservation and the Actors Fund. She also serves as a judge for the Peabody Awards.

Jennifer Siebel Newsom is a filmmaker, CEO, advocate, thought leader, and the founder and chief creative officer of the Representation Project, a nonprofit organization that uses film and media as a catalyst for cultural transformation. Her documentaries *Miss Representation* and *The Mask You Live In* explore the ways gender norms and stereotypes negatively impact girls and boys. Married to the governor of California, Gavin Newsom, she is the first partner of California.

Soledad O'Brien is an award-winning journalist, documentarian, news anchor, and producer. She is the founder and CEO of Starfish Media Group, a multiplatform media production and distribution company dedicated to uncovering and investigating empowering stories that look at the often-divisive issues of race, class, wealth, poverty, and opportunity through personal narratives.

Sandra Day O'Connor is a retired associate justice of the Supreme Court of the United States and was the first woman justice to serve on the Supreme Court. In 2009, she founded iCivics, a website dedicated to providing creative and effective teaching tools on the subject of civic engagement.

Brittany Packnett is an award-winning activist, educator, organizer, and writer who has committed her life and career to justice. She was a fall 2018 fellow at the Harvard Kennedy School's Institute of Politics; is cofounder of Campaign Zero, a policy platform to end police violence; and is cohost of the award-winning podcast *Pod Save the People*. She currently writes a column for *Teen Vogue* called "Listen Up!"

Dolly Parton is a singer-songwriter, author, actress, and philanthropist and is the most honored female country performer of all time, having garnered eight Grammy Awards, a Lifetime Achievement Award, and more than a dozen other awards throughout her career spanning more than five decades. She founded the Dollywood Foundation, which funds the literary program Dolly Parton's Imagination Library.

Nancy Pelosi made history in 2007 when she was elected the first woman to serve as Speaker of the House of Representatives. Now in her third term as Speaker, she made history again in January 2019 when she regained her position of second in line to the presidency, the first person to do so in more than sixty years. She is the author of *Know Your Power: A Message to America's Daughters.*

Amy Poehler is an Emmy Award– and Golden Globe–winning actress, as well as a writer, producer, director, and author of *Yes Please.* She is active in women's issues and serves as ambassador for the Worldwide Orphans Foundation. Onscreen and off, Amy believes in empowering women and girls everywhere. Through her digital series *Smart Girls*, Amy continues to acknowledge and support girls who are "changing the world by being themselves."

Ai-jen Poo is a labor activist, organizer, and author. She is the director of the National Domestic Workers Alliance and codirector of the Caring Across Generations campaign. She is a 2014 recipient of the MacArthur Foundation's "Genius Grant" and the author of *The Age of Dignity: Preparing for the Elder Boom in a Changing America.*

Natalie Portman in an Academy Award– and Golden Globe–winning actress who has appeared in more than forty films.

In 2004 and 2005, she traveled to Uganda, Guatemala, Ecuador, and Mexico as the ambassador of hope for FINCA International, an organization that promotes microlending to empower women in poor countries by helping them start their own businesses.

Cathy McMorris Rodgers is a Republican US representative serving the people of Washington's Fifth Congressional District since 2005. She is the only woman in history to give birth three times while serving in Congress. She is an advocate for people with disabilities.

Ileana Ros-Lehtinen is a former Republican congresswoman who served Florida's Twenty-Seventh Congressional District from 1989 to 2019. She was the first Latina elected to the US Congress and the first Republican in Congress to publicly support marriage equality. She is currently a Distinguished Presidential Fellow at the University of Miami.

Sheryl Sandberg is the chief operating officer of Facebook and founder of the Sheryl Sandberg & Dave Goldberg Family Foundation, a nonprofit organization that works to build a more equal and resilient world through two key initiatives, LeanIn .org and OptionB.org. She is the author of *Lean In: Women, Work, and the Will to Lead* and coauthor of *Option B: Facing Adversity, Building Resilience, and Finding Joy.*

Symone D. Sanders is a strategist, communications consultant, champion for women, and CNN political commentator, and she served as a spring 2018 resident fellow at the Harvard Kennedy School's Institute of Politics. She rose to prominence during her tenure as national press secretary for US Senator Bernie Sanders's presidential campaign. She is currently a senior advisor to Joe Biden and principal of the 360 Group LLC.

Maria Shriver is a Peabody Award– and Emmy Award–winning journalist and producer, an NBC News special anchor, and founder of the Women's Alzheimer's Movement, Shriver Media, and *Maria Shriver's Sunday Paper*. She is also the author of seven *New York Times* bestselling books, including her most recent title, *I've Been Thinking . . .*

Rachel Simmons is a bestselling author, educator, and consultant who helps girls and women be more authentic, assertive, and resilient. She is currently the director of the Phoebe Reese Lewis Leadership Program at Smith College. She is also the cofounder of the national nonprofit organization Girls Leadership and the author of *Odd Girl Out, The Curse of the Good Girl*, and *Enough as She Is.*

Anna Deavere Smith is an actress, playwright, teacher, and author. Smith costars on the ABC/Shonda Rhimes series *For the People* and appears on the hit ABC series *Black-ish*. Her most recent play and film, *Notes from the Field*, looks at the vulner-ability of youth, inequality, the criminal justice system, and con-temporary activism. She is the founding director of the Institute on the Arts and Civic Dialogue at New York University, where she is also a professor at NYU Tisch School of the Arts.

Olympia Snowe served as a Republican US senator for Maine from 1995 to 2013 and was known for working across party lines during her time there. Before her election to the Senate, she represented Maine's Second Congressional District in the US House of Representatives for sixteen years.

Gloria Steinem is a renowned writer, speaker, and feminist activist. In 1972, she cofounded *Ms.* magazine, which has become a landmark in both women's rights and American journalism. She also cofounded the Women's Media Center—an organization that works to raise the visibility and decision-making power of women and girls in the media—as well as Equality Now, Donor Direct Action, and the National Women's Political Caucus. Her books include the bestsellers *My Life on the Road, Revolution from Within, Outrageous Acts and Every-day Rebellions*, and *Moving Beyond Words*.

Loung Ung is a survivor of Cambodia's killing fields and is a bestselling author, activist, and cowriter of a screenplay for a 2017 Netflix original movie directed by Angelina Jolie based on her memoir, *First They Killed My Father*.

Jessica Valenti is a feminist author, Medium columnist, and cofounder and former executive director of the award-winning blog *Feministing*. Her most recent book, *Sex Object: A Memoir*, was a *New York Times* bestseller.

Diane von Fürstenberg is a fashion designer, author, and philanthropist best known for designing the iconic wrap dress in 1974. An active philanthropist, she sits on the board of Vital Voices, an organization that empowers emerging women leaders, and also serves as a director of the Diller–von Furstenberg Family Foundation, through which she has donated to several important causes.

Cleo Wade is a poet and artist and the author of the bestselling book *Heart Talk: Poetic Wisdom for a Better Life*. As seen in her 2018 TED Talk "Want to Change the World? Start by Being Brave Enough to Care," her work speaks to our collective power to create change through self-care, beloved community building, and social justice. She has been named one of America's 50 Most Influential Women by *Marie Claire* and "The Millennial Oprah" by *New York* magazine.

Alice Walker is a bestselling author of many volumes of poetry, powerful nonfiction collections, and literary fiction, and she was the first African American woman to win a Pulitzer Prize for Fiction with her novel *The Color Purple*, which also won the National Book Award. She is an activist who has worked to address problems of injustice, inequality, and poverty.

Kerry Washington is an activist, producer, and award-winning actress known for starring in ABC's hit TV drama *Scandal*, several movies, and, most recently, in *American Son* on Broadway. She is active in many social and political causes. In 2013, she was honored with the NAACP President's Award, which recognized her special achievements in furthering the causes of civil rights and public service.

Maxine Waters is a Democratic US representative serving the people of California's Forty-Third Congressional District since 1991. She made history as the first woman and first African American chair of the House Financial Services Committee. She has gained a reputation as a fearless and outspoken advocate for women, children, people of color, and the poor.

Jody Williams, a lifelong advocate for freedom and civil rights, received the Nobel Peace Prize in 1997 for her work to ban land mines. She is cofounder and chair of the Nobel Women's Initiative, which amplifies the work of grassroots women's organizations and movements around the world. She holds the Sam and Cele Keeper Endowed Professorship in Peace and Social Justice at the Graduate College of Social Work at the University of Houston, where she has been teaching since 2003. She is the author of *My Name Is Jody Williams: A Vermont Girl's*

Winding Path to the Nobel Peace Prize, her memoir on life as a grassroots activist.

Marianne Williamson is an internationally acclaimed author, spiritual leader, lecturer, activist, and teacher. Many of her books have been *New York Times* bestsellers, including the popular title *A Return to Love.* Her latest book is *A Politics of Love: A Handbook for a New American Revolution.* She previously ran for office in 2014 as an independent candidate to represent California's Thirty-Third Congressional District. In January 2019, she announced that she is running for president in 2020.

Marie Wilson, an advocate of women's issues for more than forty years, is the founder and president emerita of the White House Project and a pioneer in advancing women's leadership in every sphere—political and social, cultural and economic. She is also the former president of the Ms. Foundation for Women, where she cocreated Take Our Daughters and Sons to Work Day. She chairs the advisory board of VoteRunLead.

Oprah Winfrey is a media mogul, philanthropist, actress, producer, and author. For twenty-five years, she was the host and supervising producer of the top-rated, award-winning *Oprah Winfrey Show.* She also created the Oprah Winfrey Network (OWN); *O, The Oprah Magazine;* and the Oprah Winfrey Leadership Academy for Girls in South Africa.

Julie Zeilinger is the founding editor of WMC FBomb, a feminist media platform of the Women's Media Center for teens and young adults. She is the author of *College 101: A Girl's Guide to Freshman Year* and *A Little F'd Up: Why Feminism Is Not a Dirty Word.*

⇒ ACKNOWLEDGMENTS ⇐

I am incredibly grateful to have interviewed so many truly extraordinary thought leaders, many of whom are featured in this book, who have individually and collectively contributed to so much transformative change in the world. Those interviews and interactions have guided me, and I continue to channel and use the wisdom I have gained. This book is a way of honoring and celebrating all the powerful words of hope, insight, and inspiration of these leaders so their words can further inspire and propel change.

I am also thankful to all the many colleagues and partners who have mentored, collaborated with, and supported me and my work throughout the years.

I would like to thank Simon & Schuster and Tiller Press, which has been a wonderful and supportive home for this project, and, in particular, Lauren Hummel, who offered insightful and helpful suggestions, edits, and encouragement along the way, as well as to Theresa DiMasi and Anja Schmidt for believing in this book from the beginning and for all they did to make it possible.

And I am deeply grateful to my friend and longtime brilliant editor Angela Joshi. She and I met when we worked together on my first book, *Daring to Be Ourselves*, and I asked her to work with me on my second book, *What Will It Take to Make a Woman President?* It has been a blessing to work with her again on this book as well. Because she has worked with me on every book and on so many of the interviews and articles I have written over the years, she knows the catalog of my interviews better than anyone. So when it came to doing this book and helping to select quotes, organize them into chapters, and edit them down to their most potent distillment, she was invaluable. I simply could not have done this book without her. More than that, she is always so wonderful to work with. I feel incredibly lucky to have her as a partner in all my work.

I also want to send love and thanks to my parents, Norman and Carol Schnall, who have nurtured, encouraged, and cared for me in so many important and vital ways.

I am also forever grateful for my husband and soul mate, Tom Kay, who is such a loving and supportive life partner and an incredible father to our two daughters. And to my remarkable powerhouse daughters, Lotus and Jazmin: I love you beyond words and learn from you both every day. It has been my honor to be your mother and watch you grow into the extraordinary young women you both are, and I could not be more proud of you.

And to all those who are reading this book: Whether you are a girl yourself, or someone who cares about and supports girls, thank you for all you are doing as an agent of change. Individually and collectively, we can all make a difference.

ABOUT THE AUTHOR

Marianne Schnall is a widely published writer and interviewer whose work has appeared in a variety of media outlets, including *O, The Oprah Magazine*, TIME.com, Forbes, CNN .com, Refinery29, the Women's Media Center, the *Huffington Post*, and many others. Schnall is the founder of Feminist.com, a leading women's website and nonprofit organization, and WhatWillItTake.com, a media and event platform that engages women everywhere to advance in all levels of leadership and take action. She is the author of *What Will It Take to Make a Woman President?, Daring to Be Ourselves*, and her new book, *Leading the Way: Inspiring Words for Women on How to Live and Lead with Courage, Confidence, and Authenticity.*

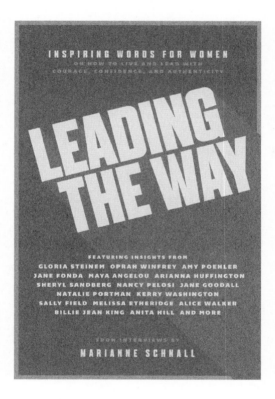